the eatgood revival

the Eatgood Revival

By

holly finlay

and

judy wallace

illustrated by holly wilkinson finlay

hastings house · publishers · new york

* * *

Published simultaneously in Canada by
Saunders of Toronto, Ltd., Don Mills, Ontario
Library of Congress Catalog Card Number: 76-39821

* * *

Library of Congress Cataloging in Publication Data

Finlay, Holly Wilkinson.
The eatgood revival.

1. Cookery. I. Wallace, Judy, joint author.
II. Title.
TX715.F5 641.5 76-39821
ISBN 0-8038-1905-6
ISBN 0-8038-1908-0 (pbk.)

* * *

Printed in the United States of America

CONTENTS

FOR MICHAEL
WHO EATS DIRT

INTRODUCTION

Throughout the country there is a growing subculture of people, mostly young, who are pulling away from the mainstream culture of plastics and instant gratification. They are the craftsmen and artists, the earth people living close to the land, the college students who have fled the dormitories to places of their own, the backpacking wanderers crisscrossing continents and sampling a variety of living styles and eating styles.

Whoever they are and wherever they are, they're all eating in a special way: they have to keep the cost low and the nourishment high, with some creativity thrown in; they want food worthy of whatever little time, effort, and money go into it.

These cooks are showing us that, on the one hand, we can spurn tasteless instant meals and dead convenience foods for far better fare, and, on the other hand, we can spurn haute or even semi-haute cuisine, which is usually too costly, too elaborate, and often too wasteful of good nutritious elements. Between the two is a whole area of REALFOOD: real taste, real nutrition, real fun in the creating. The time of THE EATGOOD REVIVAL has come.

We know that making the transition from plastic food to healthy food can be a discouraging period, if bone meal and seaweed don't appeal to you yet. We've done our best to keep the recipes in THE

EATGOOD REVIVAL as nutritious as possible without sacrificing good taste. If it doesn't taste good, nobody will want to cook it or eat it.

We have included in THE EATGOOD REVIVAL our own long-time favorites, and recipes begged from friends, and "receipts" taken from great-grandmothers' cooking notebooks from a time when food and life were generally simpler and more wholesome.

We've offered food that we consider valuable to body and mind with respect to the health and function of both.

Remember, "It's not so much what you eat, as what you balance on..." *

* Donovan, "Open Road."

HELPFUL HINTS

In this book we have used some terms and abbreviations which may possibly confuse you without some sort of explanation. Please read the following list of suggestions and advice carefully.

- Please make sure you bake at the specified temperature.
- C. stands for cup, T. for Tablespoon, t. for teaspoon.
- Always pack brown sugar firmly when measuring.
- Butter may be substituted for margarine and vice versa.
- Stock is liquid made from water in which vegetables and/or meats have been cooked. The water you use when you cook vegetables should be saved, as it contains valuable nutrients. Keep it in the refrigerator and use it often.
- Whole wheat flour (also soy, cottonseed, and peanut flour) contains a small amount of fat. It should be kept in a cool place and used frequently so it doesn't become rancid. The same goes for wheat germ, which should be kept in the refrigerator.

❀ Soybeans are an excellent meat substitute and have about three times more protein than other beans. Soy grits are soybeans broken into small pieces.

❀ Remember that hot cooked foods and cold cooked foods are equal in nutritional value.

❀ A brief discussion about honey:

Buy pure, plain honey (no additives). The darker the color is, the more strongly flavoured it will be. If your honey becomes crystallized (this happens sometimes after being stored for a long time at room temperature) you can re-liquefy it by putting the container in a pan of hot water (not over 160° or you'll ruin the flavour). If your comb honey gets squashed or something, it can also be put in a pan which is then put in hot water. The wax will float to the top and can be removed and the honey strained into a clean jar.

Honey can be substituted cup for cup with sugar when you make puddings, breads, or muffins, but remember that honey is almost twice as sweet as sugar. Honey attracts moisture, and baked things will stay fresh much longer and may even be better-tasting after a day or so. They will also be a little browner in color. If you use honey for cakes and cookies, use 7/8 c. honey for each cup of sugar called for, and reduce the liquids in the recipe by 3 T. for each cup of honey used.

Experiment — Have fun ❀

TOASTED SEEDS

SUNFLOWER, SQUASH, OR PUMPKIN

Only the sunflower seeds need to be washed; just wipe the fibers off the squash or pumpkin seeds.

Coat with 3 T. mixed oil and butter and spread out on a cookie sheet.

* Sprinkle with salt and bake at 300° for about 30-45 minutes, stirring often to toast all sides.

ROASTED SOYBEANS

Wash and soak 3 cups of soybeans over night in enough water to cover.

Drain and remove skins. Pat with towels to dry as much as possible.

Spread on cookie sheet and bake at 350° just until dry.

Heat 1" of fat to 350° in a frying pan and add soybeans. Let them cook about 10 minutes until golden.

Drain on paper towels and sprinkle with salt.

BEEF JERKY

about 3 lbs. flank steak
1 c. brown sugar
½ c. soy sauce
4 T. whiskey
½ onion, minced

Cut flank steak into long, very thin strips. Cut away any fat and discard.

Mix together sugar, soy sauce, whiskey, and onion – stir until sugar has dissolved.

Marinate meat strips in soy sauce mixture for <u>at least</u> 1 hour. Turn + stir often to coat all sides of meat.

Drain and pat dry very lightly and spread in a single layer on a baking sheet.

✿ Bake at around 300° for about an hour, turning frequently. The point is to dry out the meat as much as possible, so it may take longer depending on the thickness of the meat.

Good for hiking and good for snacks – keep in the refrigerator.

TED'S GRANOLA

- rolled oats
- wheat germ
- sesame seeds
- coconut
- brown sugar
- salt
- vanilla

} mix in any proportion you want

Add a little sesame or soy oil to sop up the "dust". Toast in a low 250°-300° oven on a greased cookie sheet for about 25 or 30 minutes or until brown. Stir occasionally to keep from burning.

Another version of cereal calls for:

3 c. rolled oats	2 T. oil
½ c. wheat germ	2 T. honey
¼ c. rice polish	2 T. brown sugar
1 c. chopped almonds	½-1 c. raisins
½ c. hulled sunflower seeds	

These measurements are all approximate. Mix everything (except the raisins) together. Don't use too much of the liquid ingredients — the mixture should be quite dry. Toast on a large, lightly greased cookie sheet at 325° for 20 minutes. Stir about every 5 minutes. Add raisins at the end (they burn).

CRUNCHY FRUITOLA

MAKES ABOUT 2 ½ QUARTS

1 ½ c. whole wheat flour
1 ½ c. quick rolled oats
2 c. sesame seeds
1 ½ c. rye flour
1 ½ c. wheat germ
1 c. ground almonds
1 c. ground dried apricots
½ c. ground dried peaches or apples
½ c. ground raisins
1 t. salt
½ c. honey
½ c. boiling water
½ c. oil

Mix all the dry stuff together.

Mix all the wet stuff together.

Then (you need 2 people for this part): One stirs the dry stuff while the other stirs the wet stuff and dribbles it into the other bowl. Rub between hands to crumble.

Spread out on a large cookie sheet and bake at 250° about 2 hours, until golden brown. Stir frequently during baking so it doesn't stick together and burn.

Cool and store in an air-tight container or in the refrigerator if you want to keep it several weeks.

BAR-LE-DUC

saltine crackers
cream cheese
a little milk
sun-cooked strawberries (p. 162)

Mash cream cheese together with a small amount of milk in order to achieve a spreading consistency.

Spread some cream cheese on a cracker, top with a dab of sun-cooked strawberries and enjoy...

✻ This makes a delicious, quick and easy light dessert and is very satisfying when you have the old munchies.

CLAM CHOWDER

SERVES 6-8

4-5 potatoes (about 3 ½ c.)
2 cans minced clams or baby clams (or 1 quart shucked steamers and their broth)
½ large onion, minced (or 1 whole small one)
salt to taste
fresh pepper to taste
1 bottle clam juice (opt.)
about 4 c. scalded milk
⅛ lb. salt pork (or about a 1½" cube)
pinch of mace

Peel and cube potatoes and put into a large kettle. Add the juice from the cans of clams and enough water to just cover potatoes. (If you use a bottle of clam juice you won't need much water.)

Add salt and pepper, mace and minced onion. Simmer, covered, until potatoes are almost tender. Lightly mash some of the potatoes to thicken the broth a bit.* Add the clams.

Scald the milk and add to the clams and potatoes. Stir, adjust seasonings to taste.

Dice salt pork into tiny dice and cook slowly in a skillet until the scraps are crisp and brown.

Add to chowder . . . they float!

* A couple T. instant potato is also a good

broth thickener— stir thoroughly.

* Don't leave chowder unrefrigerated for too long, especially in a warm place. It should really be refrigerated immediately if you don't intend to eat it right away. The longer you wait, the better it will taste...

* Before scalding milk or cream, rinse the saucepan in water; this helps to prevent a milk film from sticking to the pan.

CORN CHOWDER

SERVES 4-6

4 medium potatoes, peeled and cubed
1 medium onion, minced
3/4 t. salt
pepper to taste
12 oz. can whole kernel corn
9 oz. (approx.) can cream style corn
3 c. milk

Put potatoes, onions, salt, pepper, and liquid from can of whole kernel corn into a large pot. Add water to cover.

Simmer until potatoes are tender. Stir in both cans of corn.

Scald milk and add to pot. Adjust seasonings.

You can float salt pork scraps on top (as in Clam Chowder, p. 7) or try just a pat of margarine or butter.

* A hunk of peeled, raw potato added to chowder, soup, rice, etc., will absorb excess salt if you've overdone it in the seasoning department...... remove hunk before serving.

FRENCH ONION SOUP

SERVES 6

6 T. margarine
1 ½ lbs. thinly sliced onions
1 t. salt
3 T. cornstarch
8 c. beef broth
French bread
1 c. grated swiss cheese

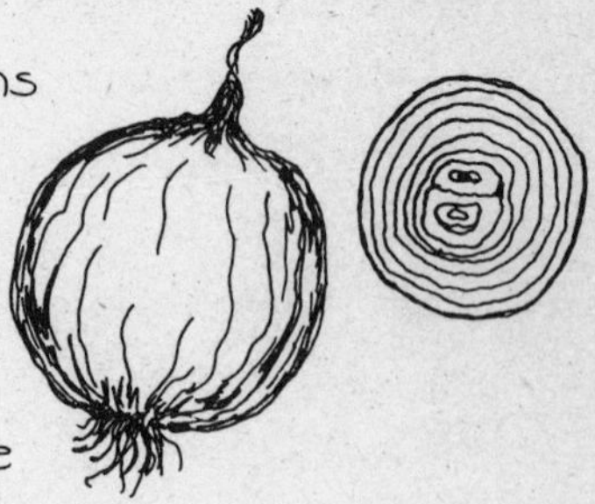

Melt margarine in a large pot. Add onions and salt and cook over medium heat until dark golden brown. (About 20 minutes.)

Blend cornstarch into a small amount of broth, then pour it, and the rest of the broth, into the pot. Cover and simmer another 40 minutes.

Slice French bread in 1-inch thick slices, rub with cut clove of garlic (or sprinkle with garlic powder), and toast on both sides.

Pour soup into an oven-proof casserole. Top with toasted French bread, sprinkle on grated cheese, and put under the broiler until cheese is bubbly.

MOM'S VEGETABLE BEEF SOUP

2 lbs. lean stew beef, cut into small chunks as for beef stew.

1 shin bone

2-3 large potatoes, peeled and chunked

2 onions, diced

½ large head of cabbage (or 1 small head), chopped or shredded

1 large tin tomatoes

pepper, salt, brown sugar to taste

Cook meat and bone in a small amount of water, with salt and pepper, in a soup kettle, until meat is tender. A pressure cooker speeds up this part.

Add remaining ingredients and bring to a boil, then reduce heat to simmer. Adjust seasoning. When potatoes are almost tender, add rivvels which take about 10 minutes to cook tender.

RIVVELS

Put 2 or 3 T. flour into a small bowl.

Add a little salt, and then add a very little bit of water, mixing with a fork.

Add more water slowly if necessary, until

you can handle the dough.

Pull the dough apart into tiny pieces, dropping them into the simmering soup as you go.

* This recipe dates back at least a hundred years. No fancy herbs are called for and none are needed. Both the bone and the cabbage are absolutely necessary to the fullness of flavour, although the soup doesn't taste at all cabbagey It's good the first day, even better the second or third, which is true of most soups, chowders, and stews.

HUNTER'S STEW

1 can condensed Cream of Pea soup
1 can condensed Cream of Tomato soup
1 can condensed Scotch Broth
1 soup can of milk
3 T. Sherry (opt.)

Empty pea soup into a large saucepan.
Add tomato soup, stirring until well blended.
Add scotch broth.
Stir milk into the combined soups, using a soup can for a measure.
Heat.
Add sherry (if desired) just before serving.

* The order of mixing the ingredients is important. Tomato soup goes into pea soup much more easily than vice versa.

This is a hearty soup. It can be served as a main course for lunch or for a light Sunday supper with salad and French bread.

SUPER STEW

2 T. cooking oil
1 lb. boneless lean beef, cubed
2 T. honey
2 t. wine vinegar
3/4 c. dry red wine
2 c. beef broth
2 T. salt
1/4 c. water
1 T. cornstarch
1/2 t. pepper
2 med. onions, diced
1 lb. fresh mushrooms, sliced
2 large carrots, cut in 1/2" pieces
3 med. potatoes, peeled & cut in 1/2" cubes
3 stalks celery, diced
1 T. margarine
1 medium rutabaga, peeled & diced
1 bay leaf

Heat 1 T. oil in frying pan. Add beef and cook over medium heat until browned. Add honey and wine vinegar and cook 2 minutes, stirring.

Transfer meat and juices to a large (6 qt.) pot or casserole with cover.

Add wine, broth, salt, and pepper to frying

pan and bring to a boil, scraping up the drippings in the bottom of the pan. Pour into casserole with meat.

Add the other T. of oil to the frying pan & cook the diced onion until translucent. Stir into casserole.

Add the diced potatoes, the rutabaga, and the bay leaf. Stir gently.

* Bake, covered, at 375° for 45 minutes.

Dice carrots and celery, stir into casserole. Refrigerate overnight. This "marries" the flavours and congeals whatever fat there may be.

The next day, skim off the fat and reheat the stew on top of the stove.

Sauté the sliced mushrooms with the margarine until almost tender.

Mix 1/4 c. water with 1 T. cornstarch and stir into stew along with sautéed mushrooms.

If liquid has become too low, stir in more wine or broth. Taste for seasoning; potatoes absorb lots of salt.

* Return to oven, covered, for 20 minutes at 350°, or until carrots are tender.

Adjust seasonings, remove bay leaf.

MARINATED MUSHROOMS

¾-1 lb. fresh button mushrooms
2 T. lemon juice
¼ c. olive oil
½ c. cider vinegar, less 2 T.
1 T. minced parsley
½ t. salt
½ t. sugar
⅛ t. pepper
1 T. tarragon (or oregano)
1 T. minced onion
1 clove minced garlic

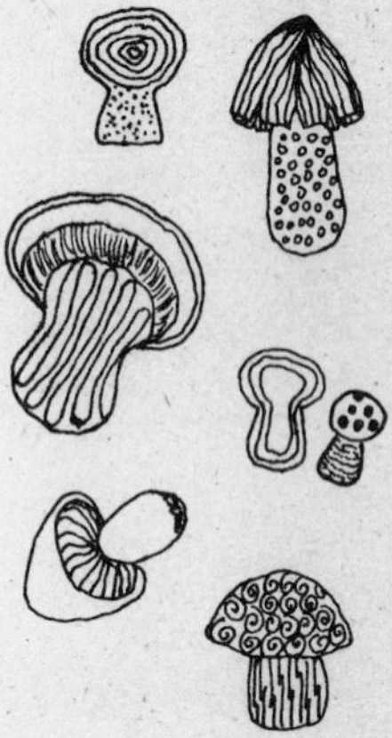

Trim stems of mushrooms and wipe off any dirt. Place in a large saucepan, cover with water, add lemon juice and stir a couple times — bring to a boil, lower heat and simmer 1 minute. Drain

Combine remaining ingredients and pour over mushrooms.

Put into clean jars and keep in refrigerator. These can also be packed in clean (sterilized) jars and sealed if you don't want to eat them right away

* You can strain the marinade, add more oil, and use as a salad dressing.

AVOCADO AND MANDARIN ORANGE SALAD

1 ripe avocado
1 small can mandarin orange segments
lettuce
French dressing
about 1 T. mandarin orange juice (from can)

Peel avocado and cut into cubes.
Add orange segments, but SAVE SOME JUICE.
Add lettuce.
Mix the mandarin orange juice with French dressing. Pour over salad.
Toss lightly to avoid mashing up the avocado.

* This is the perfect salad for any curry dish.

CUCUMBERS WITH SOUR CREAM

SERVES 6

4 large cucumbers
2 t. salt
1/4 c. wine vinegar
1/2 t. paprika
2 T. oil
1/4 c. sour cream

Peel the cucumbers and slice very thin. Sprinkle with salt and let stand 20 minutes.

Drain and press out the moisture. Add vinegar and paprika and keep in refrigerator until just before ready to serve.

Sprinkle the oil on top of the cucumbers, stir in the sour cream, and serve immediately.

FARMER'S SALAD

This is a mixture of cooked and raw vegetables which are combined in any proportions and any combinations you want.

The cooked vegetables can be:

whole kernel corn
green beans
wax beans
carrots
beets
broccoli
cauliflower
green peas

The raw portions can be:

lettuce
cucumber
sprouts
broccoli or cauliflower tips
radishes
chives

Slice, dice, and shred the vegetables into a large bowl in whatever proportions and mixtures you fancy. Dress with a mixture of salad dressing and yogurt, or mayonnaise and French dressing, or any combination thereof.

Top with crumbled bits of crisp bacon.

* This is the perfect salad in which to use up leftovers.

POTATO SALAD

7 boiled potatoes, peeled, cubed, and warm
1 walnut-sized onion, minced
1/3 cucumber, peeled and diced
1 large stalk celery, minced
1/2 green pepper, diced
} any combination

Put the above ingredients in a large bowl.

In a small bowl, mix the following ingredients together and add to the warm potatoes:

1/4 c. vinegar
1 t. celery seeds
1/2 t. dry mustard
2 T. sugar (or 3 T. maple syrup)
1/4 t. black pepper
1/2 t. salt
1 sweet pickle, minced
OR 3 sweet gherkins, minced
Mayonnaise or salad dressing to taste
French dressing—about 3 T.—optional

Mix all the ingredients well, then TASTE. It should be quite slurpy, rather than too dry.

SHRIMP SALAD

2 tomatoes, cut into wedges
lettuce, torn into pieces
2 eggs, hard-cooked and chopped
1 avocado, peeled and cut into pieces
½ cucumber, cut into small cubes
2 medium stalks of celery, diced
1 can of tiny shrimps
chopped scallion tops, chives, or small spanish onion

Put everything into a large salad bowl.
Dress with a mixture of:

French or Italian dressing
mayonnaise

This is a very filling salad and can almost stand alone as a meal for lunch or a light supper.
Sprouts can be added for extra flavour and nutrition.

FRENCH DRESSING

MAKES 1 CUP

In a 1-cup measure put the following ingredients:

- ½ c. vinegar
- ½ c. oil
- 1½ t. wet mustard
- 1 T. minced onion
- salt, pepper, sugar — a dash of each

Stir together. Pour into a jar with a top and shake well. Keep in the refrigerator and shake well before each use.

To keep your salad fresh and crisp and to keep in all the goodness, the oil part of the dressing should really be added first, before the vinegar and herbs and salt. The reasons for dressing a salad this way are good ones: when all the greens are thoroughly but lightly coated with oil, the salt won't make them go limp; the oil seals in the vitamins, minerals, and flavours because air can't get to the leaves (oxygen destroys goodness through enzyme action); and the oil distributes the seasonings evenly. If you want to dress your salads this way, toss (thoroughly) with 1 T. oil for a salad for 4, then add some of the above dressing. Serve as soon as possible.

MAPLE SYRUP DRESSING

ENOUGH FOR A SALAD FOR 2-3

4 T. mayonnaise or salad dressing
1 T. apple juice, orange juice, or other fruit juice.
1 t. maple syrup, or to taste

Mix ingredients together thoroughly. Thin with more juice if desired.

The amounts of ingredients are approximate and can be altered to suit your preference.

Serve on a Waldorf-type salad (chopped apples, nuts, carrots, celery, raisins, lettuce) or any other fruit salad you want.

ORANGE YOGURT DRESSING

ENOUGH FOR 2 OR 3

2 T. plain yogurt
2 T. salad dressing or mayonnaise
1 t. concentrated orange juice
½-1 t. honey, or to taste
grated orange rind (opt.)

Combine all ingredients and blend well. You don't have to be all that careful about the measurements — just make sure you taste it as you go along.

Serve on apples and celery salad, pear or peach halves, pineapple rings, grapefruit and orange sections or a salad of sliced apples, oranges, Bermuda onion rings, and lettuce.

* A really quick and sneaky way to make this dressing is by using half salad dressing and half orange yogurt (such as mandarin orange). Mix thoroughly, thin with milk.

SAUCE FOR AVOCADOS

SERVES 2

1 ripe avocado (in which to put the sauce)
2 T. butter or margarine
2 T. vinegar
2 T. Worcestershire sauce
2 T. ketchup
2 T. sugar or honey

Put all the ingredients — EXCEPT THE AVOCADO — into a small saucepan.

Heat ingredients, stirring constantly, until well blended and slightly bubbly.

Serve hot in avocado halves.

* This can be adapted for use as a cocktail sauce. Add 2 T. mayonnaise to the basic avocado sauce. Stir thoroughly with a whisk. over low heat until no longer lumpy. Arrange lettuce leaves in salad bowls, add avocado cubes or slices, or baby shrimp, and top with hot sauce. Serve as an appetizer or a salad.

* HINT: 2 T. of butter or margarine is an exact cube when cut from a 1/4 lb. stick.

SWEET SALAD DRESSING

½ c. sugar
1 c. oil
⅓ c. vinegar
½ c. ketchup
½ t. salt
1 t. maple syrup
¾ t. Worcestershire sauce
½ t. lemon juice
½ medium onion, grated.

Mix above ingredients together and shake well. Serve on a tossed salad. If you have a garden or have access to a variety of fresh garden greens, Sweet Salad Dressing is perfect with them.

ALMOND-RICE PANCAKES

ENOUGH FOR 5

1 3/4 c. milk
1 egg and 1 yolk
1 c. cooked brown rice
½ c. ground almonds
1 grated apple
1 c. flour
2 t. baking powder
2 t. brown sugar
½ t. salt
2 T. oil

Put everything into a big bowl and beat just enough to mix everything together.

Melt 3 T. margarine in a skillet and pour in the batter, allowing about ¼ c. per pancake (they should be thin pancakes).

Brown on both sides and serve with applesauce or Honey Butter (p. 158).

* If you have a blender, you can put the almonds in whole, and the apple cut in quarters. Whirl everything together a few seconds (until the almonds are grated) and cook as above.

SCOTTISH CRUMPETS

2 GENEROUS SERVINGS

2 eggs, separated
1 T. & 1½ t. brown sugar
½ c. milk
½ c. flour

Beat egg whites until stiff.

Beat the egg yolks until thick and lemon-coloured, then beat in the sugar.

Stir in milk.

Gradually blend in flour.

Fold in egg whites — do this part carefully.

Cook on a hot greased skillet until golden brown, flip and do other side.

Serve warm with butter or margarine, sugar, jelly, honey, or whatever you like.

* These are like very fluffy French pancakes.

A VERY GOOD SANDWICH

FOR YOU

2 slices good rye bread
3-4 thin slices of ripe avocado
2-4 strips freshly cooked bacon
mayonnaise – 2-4 T.
lemon juice – about 1 t.

Cook bacon, drain.

Pop bread into the toaster.

Mix mayonnaise with lemon juice, taste, and adjust proportions if necessary.

Slice and peel avocado

Butter toast lightly, spread mayonnaise mixture on top, then arrange avocado and bacon on mayonnaise.

EAT... Make another one. 

EGG FOO YUNG

ENOUGH FOR 4 WITH SOMETHING ELSE. OR, ENOUGH FOR 2 HUNGRY VEGETARIANS IF YOU LEAVE OUT THE MEAT.

Sauce:
3 t. soy sauce
1 t. cornstarch
1 t. sugar
1 t. vinegar
½ c. beef broth

Egg mix:
1 c. fresh mung bean sprouts (p. 91)
1 onion, thinly sliced
4-5 strips bacon (or 1 c. clean shrimp)
6 eggs
2 T. fat

Make sauce first. Put everything into a small pan. Cook over low heat until thick.

If you're using bacon, fry it first in a small skillet until soft and brown (save the fat). Cut into small pieces and put into a bowl.

Fry onions and sprouts a few minutes in bacon fat, until onions are soft. Add to the bacon bowl.

Break eggs into bowl. Stir together with bacon, onions, and sprouts.

Pour into a hot skillet about ¼ c. at a time, and fry like small pancakes until golden brown on both sides (about 5 minutes altogether).

Serve the sauce separately.

CURRIED SCRAMBLE

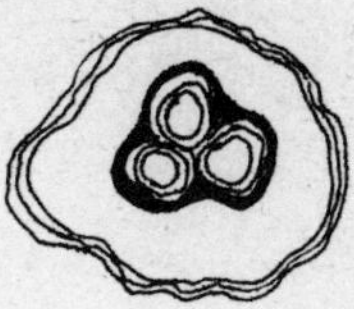

4 eggs
2 t. curry powder
1/4 c. parmesan cheese
2 T. water or cream

Break eggs into a bowl. Add everything else. Stir with a fork just to mix everything together.

Melt 4 T. margarine in a skillet.

Pour in egg mixture and stir constantly until set, but still creamy (3-5 min.).

SIMPLY SCRAMBLE

FOR 2

3 eggs
2 T. water
salt and pepper to taste
2 T. butter or margarine

Melt butter in frying pan. Stir together rest of ingredients — do not beat. When butter bubbles add egg mixture. Stir constantly with a fork just until they look like scrambled eggs — 3-6 minutes. Serve immediately.

Some herbs and other good things with eggs are:

chervil	sesame seeds
thyme (not too much)	wheat germ
parsley	chopped green pepper
chives	cooked bits of chicken
tarragon	small rounds of hot dogs

For an **OMELETTE**:

Use the same egg mixture. Pour into a preheated, buttered skillet. By using a spatula, lift edges of egg and tip pan to let uncooked part run under. Shake pan occasionally to keep egg from sticking. Add a filling if you want — chopped fresh tomatoes, sliced mushrooms, grated cheese, chopped cooked meat, sprouts, minced onion . . . Fold in half and slide onto plate.

THE FARM PEOPLE'S BASQUE OMELETTE

FOR 2

2 eggs
2 slices bread (any kind — experiment) minus crusts
2 T. milk

Soak the bread in the milk until good & mushy. Then add the eggs and beat a lot.

Pour into a small, well-greased frying pan and cook, lifting the edges to let the uncooked egg run under.

At this point you can add some other things if you want — cheese, mushrooms, peppers — and cook until bottom is golden (about 4 minutes altogether).

Then pop into a 325° oven for 5 minutes until puffy and the top is dry.

HAM AND CHEESE PUFF

SERVES 2

Mix together:

3 T. soft butter
3 egg yolks
3/4 c. grated parmesan cheese
1 c. diced, cooked ham
1 t. mustard

Then fold in 3 stiffly beaten egg whites, being careful not to deflate the whites too much. * Pour into a well-greased 8" shallow pan and bake at 350° until puffed up and light brown (about 10-12 minutes).

* With just a salad or coleslaw, this makes a really good light dinner.

TOADS-IN-HOLES

Despite its ridiculous name, this makes a very good, easy, and inexpensive meal.

1 c. flour ½ t. salt 2 eggs 1 c. milk	Beat together until very well mixed.

In a 425° oven, heat ¼ c. fat until it sizzles, in a shallow pan about 9" square.

Pour in the batter, and arrange on it as many hot dogs (or sausages) as you want, up to about 8.

✿ Bake at 425° for 30 minutes until crusty, and the holes have covered up the toads (as it were).

Serve with mustard.

TUNA PIES

This being a short dissertation on the incredible versatility of the tuna-pie maker itself. Variously manufactured under such names as QWIKI-PIE and SANWITCH-TOAST-R, the best ones are made of cast iron and have 2 sandwich molds.

The best thing about them is that they can be used over any heat source — campfire, wood stove, hotplate ..., and the cast-iron ones should not be washed (BONUS) - only wiped out and occasionally brushed out with a small wire brush.

How To Work It:

Pre-heat iron molds about 10 minutes (aluminum ones do not need to be pre-heated - they do need to be washed, however).

Butter 2 pieces of bread (4, if it's a 2-sandwich mold), place 1 piece bread buttered side toward the mold, fill with whatever you want, top with other piece of bread, butter side up toward the mold, then close. Place directly on heat and cook about 4 minutes (2 each side) for a nice toasty-grilled sandwich.

Some Things To Try:

1) 2 pieces buttered bread & tuna fish salad
2) 2 pieces buttered bread & 1 raw egg (3 minutes–

1½ each side, for a poached egg sandwich.

3) 2 whole wheat bread slices, buttered & sugared (it caramelizes) and applesauce filling

4) 2 pieces buttered bread & cheese & tomato and/or ham

5) 2 thin slices poundcake, buttered and sugared, and peaches for filling

The tuna pie maker is limited only by your imagination and the size of the mold —

✿ THINK WEIRD ✿

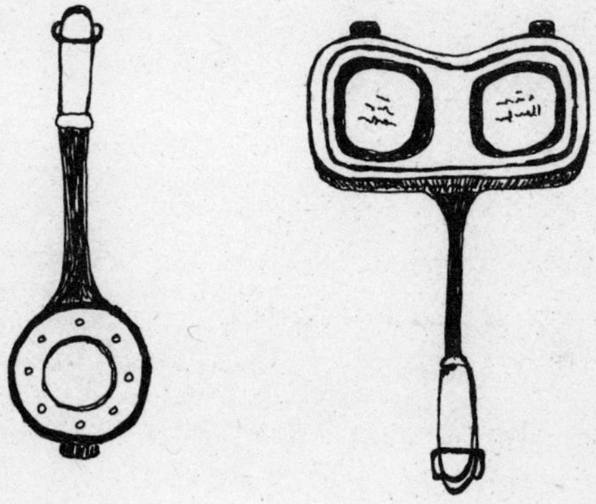

CURRIED SHRIMP

SERVES 4-6

1 large onion, minced
2-3 T. oil or margarine
½ lb. fresh mushrooms, sliced (optional, but good)
1 ripe banana, cut into tiny hunks
2 T. flour
½ c. milk
1 can cream of chicken soup
salt - to taste
brown sugar - to taste
curry powder - to taste
a very small pinch of tarragon
raisins (optional)
pre-cooked fresh, frozen, or canned shrimp

Mince the onion, slice the mushrooms, and sauté in a large frying pan in the oil or margarine.

Add the banana, flour, and milk, stirring constantly as you add the milk so the mixture won't get too lumpy.

Add the cream of chicken soup, salt, brown sugar, tarragon and curry, TASTING as you add.

Add the raisins (if you want) and mix well.

Add the shrimps and simmer about 5 minutes. Then taste for seasoning.

Serve the curry in the center of a ring of boiled rice, then add the condiments as desired. These would include such things as chutney, shredded coconut, slivered almonds, chopped peanuts or cashews, chopped green peppers, chopped pineapple, bacon bits, or chopped hard-boiled eggs.

* A small variation consists of omitting the brown sugar and the banana and adding instead some apple butter (too much, though, and it will be too sweet) and/or some diced apples.
This recipe works equally well with any kind of meat . . . shrimp, chicken, beef, pork, lamb . . . pre-cooked, of course.
You should probably plan on <u>about</u> 3 cups of meat, but don't worry about exact amounts.

SHRIMP AND RICE CASSEROLE

SERVES 6

1-2 lbs. cooked shrimp
1 T. lemon juice
3 C. cooked rice
3 T. margarine
1/4 c. minced onion
1/4 c. minced green pepper
1 can condensed tomato soup
1/2 t. salt
1/8 t. pepper
1/8 t. nutmeg or mace
1 c. light cream
1/2 c. slivered almonds.

Place shrimp in a 2-quart casserole and sprinkle with lemon juice.

Sauté the onion and green pepper in the margarine, then stir in the cooked rice. Add to the shrimp in the casserole.

Mix together the soup, salt, pepper, and nutmeg, add the cream gradually, then half the almonds. Pour this mixture over the shrimp and rice and mix gently. Sprinkle the rest of the almonds over the top.

Bake uncovered at 350° for 35-40 minutes, or until bubbly around the edges.

SHRIMP FONDUE

SERVES ABOUT 3

1 can (10 oz.) frozen condensed cream of shrimp soup
½ lb. sharp cheddar cheese in small hunks
1 t. Worcestershire sauce

Put all three ingredients in top of double boiler over boiling water.

Stir frequently until the cheese has melted and the mixture has become suitably gooey in consistency (the cheese will do this).

Thin with milk if you wish.

Serve on toast, crackers, or your choice.

SHEEPSHEAD BAY CASSEROLE

SERVES 4-6

¼ lb. fresh sliced mushrooms

½ onion, minced

½ green pepper, diced

½ c. celery, diced (about 1 large stalk)

3 T. butter or margarine

3 T. flour

2 c. milk

1 T. dried parsley

salt and pepper to taste

1 can drained, flaked crab meat (about 1 cup)

1 can tiny shrimp (1 c.)

1 c. bread crumbs

½ c. grated cheddar cheese

Melt butter in a large skillet and sauté mushrooms, onion, green pepper, and celery until almost soft. Stir in flour.

Gradually add milk and stir until it thickens slightly. Add parsley, salt, and pepper. Gently stir in sea food.

Spoon half the mixture into a buttered casserole. Add a layer of bread crumbs, then some grated cheese. Add the rest of the sea food mixture and top with a final layer of crumbs and cheese.

Bake at 450° about 20 minutes or until bubbly.

CHICKEN BREASTS WITH RICE

SERVES 2

2 breasts of chicken
flour
2 T. cooking oil
3/4 c. rice
1/2 t. salt
1/8 t. pepper
1 T. minced onion
3 T. dehydrated onion soup mix
1/4 lb. sliced fresh mushrooms (or a 3 oz. can)
1 chicken bouillon cube
1 3/4 c. boiling water
margarine or butter

Split breasts, remove breast bone. Pat dry and dust lightly with flour. Brown in oil until golden.

Combine the rice, salt, and pepper in a greased 2 quart casserole and sprinkle with the minced onion and onion soup mix. Add the mushrooms.

Arrange the breasts on top of the rice.

Dissolve the bouillon cube in the boiling water and pour over everything. Dot with margarine.

Cover and bake at 350° for 1 hour.

Real chicken stock can be used in place of the water, bouillon cube, and onion soup mix.

CHICKEN NORMANDY

Heat 6 T. margarine in a large skillet.

Add: 1 chicken – cut in pieces
2 potatoes – washed, dried, & cut in 1/4" slices
2 apples – cored and chopped
2 onions — thinly sliced

Sauté until everything is brown (about 20 min.)

Then add: 3/4 c. apple cider
1/2 c. chicken broth

Cover and simmer over low heat until chicken and potatoes are tender (30 minutes).

Add: 1/2 c. heavy cream

Stir just until heated through.

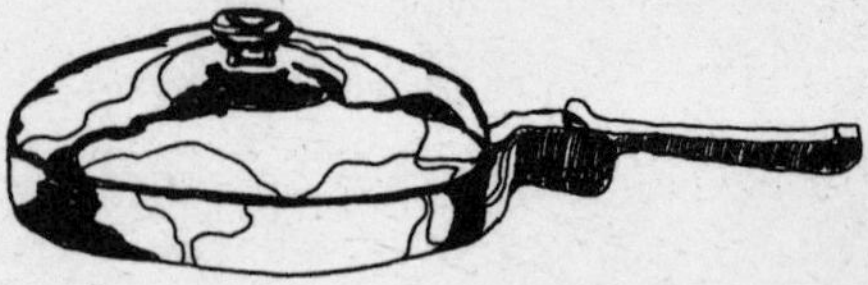

CHICKEN TARRAGON

2 whole chicken breasts, boned
1 T. dried tarragon
4 T. margarine
1 T. cornstarch
½ c. heavy cream

Pound the chicken breasts very thin between 2 pieces of saran wrap.

Melt the margarine in a frying pan over medium-high heat; then lay in the chicken pieces and sprinkle them with the tarragon.

Cook just until light brown (about 5 min. on each side).

Stir the cream into the cornstarch, then pour it over the chicken and stir just until thickened (about 3 minutes).

✱ You should serve this over brown rice or something to catch the sauce.

GREASELESS FRIED-TASTING CHICKEN

chicken pieces – as many as you think you can eat

evaporated milk, or whole milk with an egg beaten into it

Bisquick or other similar biscuit mix

Dip the pieces of chicken in the milk, then dip them in the Bisquick enough to coat them LIGHTLY. Sauté the coated pieces in butter or margarine until light golden brown, then transfer to a greased baking sheet or roasting pan. Arrange in a single layer.

Bake at 350° for about an hour, turning occasionally (once or twice will do). Pierce with a fork to check for tenderness. Meat should offer little resistance to fork when done.

LEMON CHICKEN

chicken pieces for 4 people
½ c. lemon juice
½ onion, minced
½ c. sour cream
1 c. fine bread crumbs
salt and pepper

Combine lemon juice and onion and marinate chicken pieces at least 1 hour—be sure all sides are exposed to marinade by turning, if necessary.

Remove from lemon juice, salt and pepper each piece, then dip in sour cream. Coat with bread crumbs.

Put on a lightly greased cookie sheet and bake 30 minutes at 400° (time is slightly less if you're using only breasts); turn up heat to 450° and cook an extra 15 minutes or until tender and slightly browned.

Good hot and good cold.

ROAST CHICKEN

1 chicken, 2-4 pounds
3/4 lb. fresh mushrooms
1/2 stick butter or margarine
fresh parsley
rosemary

Prepare chicken for roasting.

Do not salt. This draws out the juices and you don't want that to happen in this case.

CAREFULLY lift the skin over the breasts, gently separating it from the flesh as far back toward the neck end as you can without ripping the skin. The exact area is indicated on the chicken drawing, between the dotted lines. This is actually easier than it sounds because the skin isn't attached that securely.

Now trim off the very ends of about 6 clean mushrooms and slice the mushrooms lengthwise into fairly thin pieces. 

Carefully slide the mushroom slices, alternating with pats of margarine or butter, into the space you have just made between the flesh and the skin. Fit as much as you can in the space available, slicing more mushrooms if necessary.

Sprinkle rosemary in the cavity of the chicken where the stuffing normally goes.

Chop up the parsley, perhaps 1/3 - 1/2 cup, and toss lightly with the whole mushrooms. Put this mixture into the chicken cavity.

Place bird in roasting pan and tie legs together if necessary.

The chicken will look lumpy ... of course.

* Bake at 350° until the leg joint moves easily.

No basting is necessary.

* A whole peeled onion can be substituted for the mushroom/parsley mixture.

ROSEMARY CHICKEN

2 lbs. chicken parts (or as many as you think you'll need)
½ stick margarine (¼ c.)
1 can condensed mushroom soup
⅓ c. sherry
dash of freshly ground pepper
10 (or so) fresh small white onions
rosemary

Melt margarine in largish covered skillet. Brown chicken pieces in margarine, salt lightly while browning.
Mix together the soup, sherry, and pepper.
Pour it over the chicken.
Add onions.
Sprinkle rosemary over all.
* Cover tightly and simmer about 45 min. until chicken is tender.

* Once this is all together and gently simmering along, you can almost forget it. It takes very little attention . . . just don't _totally_ forget!

SAUTÉED CHICKEN WITH ARTICHOKE HEARTS

SERVES 2-4

This is a fantastic combination ... if the thought of artichoke hearts and shallots makes you clutch at your wallet, don't forget that chicken is so inexpensive that it's really worth it.

2 chicken breasts, 4 legs, or any combination at all
Salt
pepper

4 T. margarine
2 T. oil
1-2 doz. shallots (tiny white onions will do in a pinch)
2 bay leaves
1 pkg. frozen artichoke hearts or 1 can of same
(not marinated)
2 T. margarine (for the artichoke hearts)
1 t. lemon juice
½ c. chicken stock
chopped fresh parsley

If you're using breasts, you may want to split each one in half. At any rate, rinse the chicken pieces under cold water and dry thoroughly (they brown better when dry). Salt and pepper each piece, all sides.

Heat 4 T. margarine & 2 T. salad or vegetable

oil in a heavy frying pan until hot.

Cook the chicken over high-ish heat, a few pieces at a time, turning frequently. Remove each piece to a plate as soon as it's dark golden brown.

Peel the shallots and put in a frying pan when chicken has finished browning. Shake the pan often to prevent sticking. In about 3 minutes, or when they are golden, carefully remove them.

Pour off all but 2 T. fat in pan and return chicken to the pan. The pieces should be in one layer, with the breasts on top of the legs if necessary (they tend to cook faster than other chicken parts).

Add the browned shallots and 2 bay leaves and cover the pan.

Simmer for 30 minutes, basting every 10 minutes with pan juices.

Melt 2 T. margarine in a smallish saucepan. Add defrosted artichoke hearts (or drained, canned ones) and 1 t. lemon juice and a pinch of salt. Cover and simmer 10-15 minutes.

Arrange chicken, shallots, and artichoke hearts on a warm plate.

Add ½ c. chicken stock to juices in frying pan. Scrape up the sticky bits on the bottom of the pan and boil down to ½ cup (approximately).

Pour over the chicken and garnish with chopped fresh parsley.

SWISS CHICKEN

2 whole chicken breasts (boned)
1 stick butter
½ t. nutmeg
2 c. bread crumbs
1 c. grated swiss cheese
2 eggs, beaten
1 whole lemon, cut in wedges

Pound chicken breasts very thin between 2 pieces of saran wrap.

Mix 1 c. of crumbs with nutmeg on a plate.

Pour the beaten eggs into a flat dish.

Mix the cheese with the other cup of crumbs.

Dip the chicken breasts in the crumbs/nutmeg mixture, then into the eggs, and finally into the crumbs/cheese mixture, coating them well.

Melt the butter in a large frying pan. When bubbly, add chicken pieces and sauté until crisp and golden brown on both sides (about 10 min. each side).

Serve with lemon wedges.

TURKEY-NUT ROAST

SERVES 4

This is a really nice post-Thanksgiving dinner, but you can easily substitute ham for the turkey any time of year.

2 c. diced cooked turkey
½ lb. sliced mushrooms
1 stick butter
½ c. chopped walnuts
1 lg. chopped onion
1 8 oz. pkg. herb-seasoned Pepperidge Farm Stuffing Mix
1 c. grated Swiss cheese
5 well-beaten eggs
¼ c. bottled steak sauce

Melt the butter in a skillet and fry together the onion and mushrooms just until the onion is light brown and limp.

Pour everything in the skillet into a large bowl and add everything but the steak sauce to it. Stir well and pour into a greased casserole.

✽ Bake at 350° for 30 minutes. Mix the steak sauce with ¼ c. water, pour on top and bake 30 minutes more.

cont'd.

Serve Turkey-Nut Roast with this sauce:

1 can cream of mushroom soup, undiluted
1 cup sour cream
1 t. gravy-browner *
1/4 c. water

Heat together over low heat just until gravy starts to bubble.

* If you have no gravy-browner on hand, melt and caramelize 1 T. sugar in an old spoon directly over the burner & stir at once into the sauce — there will be no sweetness, but a good color and flavour.

* Vegetarians: leave out the meat and add more mushrooms and nuts — different taste, but just as yummy.

BAKED HAM SLICE

1 ham slice – a small ½" slice is good for 2 people, but any thickness works here

milk

brown sugar OR honey

mustard – dry or prepared

whole cloves

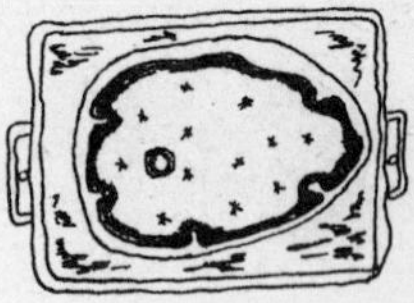

Place ham slice in a baking dish, not too much larger than the ham.

Spread a thin layer of wet mustard over top of slice, or sprinkle thin layer of dry mustard over top.

Sprinkle a thin coating of brown sugar over the mustard OR dribble honey over it all.

Stick whole cloves at approximately 1½" intervals over the surface of the ham slice.

Pour milk around the edges of the slice up almost to the level of the top of the slice, being careful not to wash away the sugar & mustard.

Bake uncovered in the oven at 350° until tender, about 30-40 minutes.

* Remember this: 1 t. dry mustard = 1 T. wet

* Some minced onion is good on ham, too.

CHEESEBURGER PIE

SERVES 4

Crust: 1 1/4 c. Pepperidge Farm Stuffing Mix (any kind)
1/4 c. melted margarine

Mix together and press into a 9" pie plate.

Filling: 1 lb. ground beef
1/2 t. oregano
1 small chopped onion
1/2 c. bread crumbs
4 oz. tomato sauce (1/2 can)*

Brown beef with onion about 5 minutes. Pour off all the fat. Mix the meat and onion with everything else, and spoon into crust.

Topping: 8 oz. grated cheddar cheese
1 egg
1/4 c. milk
1/2 t. mustard
1 t. worcestershire or soy sauce

Mix together and spread on top of meat.

* Bake pie 30 minutes at 425°.

* Sauce: Mix the other 1/2 can of tomato sauce with 1/2 c. chili sauce or ketchup. Bring just to a boil over medium heat.

STOVE-TOP MEATLOAF

SERVES 4 or 2 WITH SOME LEFT FOR SANDWICHES.

Mix together in a large bowl:

2 lbs. ground beef
1 lg. onion, chopped fine
2 cloves garlic, minced
½ c. bread crumbs
1 egg

In a large skillet melt 1 stick of margarine over medium heat. When it's bubbling, add 3 onions, thinly sliced and separated into rings. Cover and cook until soft.

Push onions together to form a bed for the meat. Lay the meat on top and pat it into a large round loaf about 2" thick.

Cook over medium heat (do not cover pan) about ½ hour until onions are crisp and brown.

Put a plate face down on loaf and invert. Slip loaf back into pan (onions are on top now) and cook another ½ hour, spooning the juices from the pan over the top of the loaf from time to time.

MUNCHY MEATLOAF

SERVES 3-4

There can be infinite subtle variations in the preparation of this meatloaf and it will almost always taste incredibly good. The ground beef and the breadcrumbs are a constant, however. Spice it up your own way if you like, but keep in mind that it should be fairly moist before cooking or it will be a very dry meatloaf in the end.

1 lb. ground beef
1 egg
1 T. dehydrated onion soup
1 small onion, minced
½ t. salt
several grinds of pepper
½ t. parsley
2 T. wheat germ
⅛ c. ketchup
¾ c. herbed bread crumbs
⅛ c. ketchup to spread on top (optional)
2-3 strips bacon to spread on top (optional)

Mix all ingredients together in a large bowl. Use your hands... it's faster and easier. Milk or tomato juice or an extra egg can be used if mixture is too dry.

✿ Press into a loaf pan & bake at 350° for about 45 minutes.

MEATBALLS AND SOUR CREAM

SERVES 4-6

MUNCHY MEATLOAF mixture
1 C. sour cream
½ c. condensed cream of chicken OR cream of mushroom soup

Form MUNCHY MEATLOAF mixture into walnut-size meatballs.

Melt about 1 T. margarine in a large frying pan and add the meatballs. Don't crowd them too much.

Cook over lowish heat turning meatballs often to prevent burning and insure even cooking.

Mix the sour cream and soup together and stir into the meatballs.

Simmer 5-10 minutes or until the sauce is mildly bubbly.

* Uncooked MUNCHY MEATLOAF mixture will keep for several days in the refrigerator so you don't have to make a million meatballs all at once. This mixture makes great meat patties and can be used for the meatball part of spaghetti.

SWEET AND SOUR MEATBALLS

Make small meatballs from Munchy Meatloaf mixture.

Cook in 2 T. margarine in a skillet over low heat, turning frequently until almost done.

Make sweet & sour sauce:

In a small pan mix: 1/2 c. sugar (brown)
2 T. cornstarch

Add: 1/2 c. vinegar
1 T. soy sauce
1 c. pineapple juice drained from a can of chunky pineapple

Cook over medium 'til bubbly.

Stir into meatballs along with pineapple chunks. Heat slowly, stirring, 'til meatballs are coated and pineapple is heated through.

Serve with rice.

WILKIEBURGERS

large rolls (onion rolls, whole Wheat Onion Buns, etc.)
ground beef
1 Bermuda onion, sliced thin
shredded lettuce
Barbecue Relish
cheese (optional)
ketchup (optional)

Split rolls, butter both halves, place each pair of halves on a square of foil (roughly 12" square).

Put a slice of Bermuda onion on bottom half of each pair.

Fry or broil large flat rounds of ground beef. Season with salt & pepper during cooking.

Put cooked beef on onion slice.

Put handful of shredded lettuce on beef.

Put Barbecue Relish on lettuce.

Put ketchup and/or cheese on Relish (optional).

Put top half of roll on top...

Pull foil up and over the burger, seal with a lock fold, fold up ends, and put into a pre-heated 300° oven for about 10 minutes.

SHEPHERD'S PIE

1 lb. ground beef
1 med. onion, minced
½ green pepper, minced
Salt & pepper to taste
2 T. butter or margarine
4 potatoes, mashed (about 2 c.)
1 pkg. mixed vegetables (or any vegetable combination)
2 T. margarine or butter
milk

Sauté onion & green pepper in 2 T. margarine.
Add ground beef and stir until browned. Season.
Cook potatoes, mash, season with salt & pepper, thin with milk if desired.
Cook vegetables, season. **Don't pour out juice.**
In casserole dish, make layers of meat and vegetables. Top with mashed potatoes, dot with margarine.
* Bake in a 325° oven for about 20 minutes or until heated through.

* This can be made a day or so ahead of time. Actually, the flavour is better on the second day.

YAM-APPLE CASSEROLE

SERVES 2

2 thinly sliced yams or sweet potatoes
2 thinly sliced, cored apples
1 small sliced onion
½ c. maple syrup
¾ c. apple cider
½ c. melted butter
6 sausages

Alternate layers of yams, apples, and onions in a greased casserole.

Combine syrup, cider, and butter and pour over the top.

* Cover the casserole and bake at 350° for 1 hr.

Then uncover, arrange sausages on top and bake ½ hour more, uncovered.

* You may want to partially cook your sausages ahead of time if you think they are apt to be quite fatty.

SPAGHETTI CASSEROLE

SERVES 6-8

1 1/4 lbs. ground beef
1 green pepper, minced
1 onion, minced
2 stalks celery, minced
2 T. margarine
8-10 oz. spaghetti
1 lg. can tomato paste
1 15 oz. can tomato sauce
1/2 t. oregano (or to taste)
dash cinnamon
salt to taste
2 T. sugar (or to taste)
1/4 lb. grated mozzarella cheese
bread crumbs

Put spaghetti on to cook.

In a large skillet, sauté onion, celery, and green pepper in margarine. Add ground beef and cook until it loses its red color.

Stir in tomato paste, tomato sauce, oregano, cinnamon, salt, and sugar. Stir, taste, and adjust seasoning if necessary — sugar will cut the tart taste. Simmer the sauce, covered, until the spaghetti is done.

Mix together the drained spaghetti and the tomato sauce. Put it in an oven-proof casserole and sprinkle bread crumbs over all. Sprinkle grated cheese evenly over crumbs.

* Bake at 350° for 25-30 minutes or until cheese has melted and casserole is heated through.

* This keeps well in the refrigerator and even improves on the second (or third!) day.

SUPER LASAGNE

This recipe is very heavy and very rich. It's enough to fill an 11 x 16 x 3" aluminum foil roasting pan and will easily feed 12 starving lasagne friends.

First you make the sauce:

4 chopped onions
2 lbs. ground beef
4 cloves garlic, minced
1/4 c. olive oil
2 T. oregano
2 t. thyme
2 t. basil
2 t. salt
5 small cans tomato paste
8 tomato paste cansful of water
2 c. dry red wine (any kind)
a handful of mushrooms
3 T. sugar

Brown onions, beef, and garlic in the olive oil for 10 minutes.

Add everything else. Cover pot and simmer over low heat for 3 hours. It makes a very thick sauce, but you can add more water as it cooks away if you want it thinner.

Meanwhile:

In one bowl mix together: 2 lbs. ricotta cheese
1 egg

Into another bowl grate: 1½ lbs. mozzarella cheese

Then:

Just before the sauce is done, fill a giant pot* with water and bring it to a boil. When it's boiling, add 2 lbs. lasagne noodles and cook 10 minutes.

When the noodles are done, drain them and return to pot. Cover with cold water to keep them from sticking together.

* If you don't have a giant pot, cook the noodles in two batches.

Now:

Spread some sauce on the bottom of your big roaster pan, then cover completely with a layer of noodles. Spread some ricotta mixture on the noodles, then sprinkle with some mozzarella. Repeat layers until everything is used up, ending with sauce. Sprinkle a lot of mozzarella cheese on top.

Bake at 375° for 30 minutes. Just before you take it out of the oven, turn on the broiler to make the top crusty and brown.

* It tastes better the second day but it'll never last long enough for you to find that out.

THE BASIC FRENCH ARTICHOKE

Allow 1 per person.

Cut off stems so they'll stand upright — then pull off the little dark leaves around the base. Wash and drain.

Boil a lot of water in a big pot. Add 1 T. oil and 1 whole clove of garlic. Stand artichokes upright in the water. Cover and cook over medium-low heat for 45 minutes (or until a leaf pulls off easily). Drain and serve.

LEMON GARLIC BUTTER

FOR 2

1 stick butter
1 clove garlic (or ½ t. garlic powder)
1 squeeze of lemon juice

Mince the garlic and brown in the melted butter. Add the lemon juice. Pour into two little bowls and serve with the artichokes for leaf dipping.

* As a tasty variation, you can also use plain sour cream for dipping.

BAKED CORN ON THE COB

Mix together in a little bowl:

½ c. soft butter
1 T. mustard
1 t. horseradish (opt.)
½ t. salt

Remove the husks and silk from 4 ears of corn and spread each ear with some of the butter mixture.

✻ Wrap each ear separately in a piece of aluminum foil and bake in a 400° oven for 20 minutes.

✻ You can cook these outside the same way. Just put the foiled corn on the coals and turn occasionally for ½ hour.

BROWN RICE

SERVES 6

1 c. natural brown rice
3 c. water or stock
1/4 t. salt

Bring water and salt to a boil.
Slowly add rice and cover pot tightly.
Simmer about 1 hour until water is absorbed and rice is tender. During this time, do not stir the rice. Set aside, leaving cover on pan, for about 15 minutes so that the rice will be fluffy.

* One cup of raw rice will equal about 3 1/2 cups rice when cooked.
Just before you serve the rice, stir in a bunch of tiny cherry tomatoes. They're good

LONG-GRAIN BROWN RICE

SERVES 3-4, OR 2 VERY HUNGRY PEOPLE

1 c. rice
2 c. water

Stir together in a pot that has a tight-fitting lid.

Bring to a boil over high heat. As soon as it starts to boil, turn heat to low, cover pot, and let simmer 45 minutes. (Don't peek or you'll have 3 cups of pebbles.)

CURRY SAUCE FOR RICE

4 T. margarine
1 onion
1 tomato
1 pepper
a few fresh mushrooms
2 T. curry powder
½ c. sour cream
½ can undiluted cream of mushroom soup

This is a very adaptable sauce. Everything listed above is optional except the curry, sour cream, and soup. Improvise as much as you like from that.

Melt the margarine in a small skillet.

Add the onion and pepper, sliced thin. Let

cook about 8 minutes, until soft.

Add chopped tomato and mushrooms. Toss around about 3 minutes.

Stir in curry to coat all the vegetables.

Add undiluted soup and let cook on low heat about 10 minutes until thick and bubbly.

Stir in sour cream and let it just get hot.

Serve over brown (or saffron) rice.

BROWN RICE CASSEROLE

Rice Part

1 1/4 c. brown rice
2 T. margarine or butter
3 c. hot chicken stock or boiling water
1/2 t. salt
1 T. minced onion

Sauté rice and onion in margarine in a saucepan until brown and popcorn-fragrant.

Add chicken stock, or water and salt, stir, cover, and simmer until done.

Vegetable Part

tomatoes (essential for juices)
celery (sliced)
green pepper (chopped)
onions (minced or sliced into rings)
zucchini squash (sliced)
broccoli
carrots (sliced)
scallions

Use any or all vegetables — whatever you have on hand.

Put cut vegetables into top of double boiler over simmering water. During cooking, add tomato paste so it's not watery.

Add seasonings to taste:

- salt
- pepper
- Tabasco (3 or 4 drops)
- thyme
- oregano
- parsley flakes
- sherry

LAST PART

Place in layers (rice, vegetables, rice, vegetables) in a buttered casserole.

Sprinkle with cheese — swiss, cheddar, or you name it.

Heat in a 350° oven for about 20 minutes.

* This is really good as the hearty portion of a vegetarian meal. It's great with yogurt, a salad, and perhaps nuts and dates.

NANCY'S BASIC VEGETARIAN EXTRAVAGANZA

SERVES 4

Cook 1½ c. brown rice at a low boil in 3 cups water until water is gone and rice is tender. (If necessary add a little more water and keep boiling.) It should take about 45 minutes.

While the rice is boiling, sauté 1 chopped onion in a little butter until soft and golden.

When rice is done, add to it:

½ c. raisins (give or take a raisin)
2 or 3 eggs (raw)
2 bananas, sliced
nuts, if you like

In a very hot frying pan, fry rice/egg/fruit mix with the onion until brown and crusty.

RICE WITH HERBS

6-8 SERVINGS

4 T. margarine
1 T. finely chopped onion
1 C. uncooked rice
½ t. dried thyme or 2 sprigs fresh
1 bay leaf
½ t. dry parsley or 2 sprigs fresh
2 drops Tabasco sauce
3 C. chicken stock

Melt 2 T. margarine in a casserole or saucepan which can go in the oven. Add onion. Cook, stirring, until onion is translucent.

Add rice and cook 3 min. longer.

Add thyme, bay leaf, parsley, Tabasco, and stock. Bring to a boil, cover tightly, and transfer to the oven.

⚘ Bake at 400° for 20 minutes or until rice is tender and fluffy.

Remove cover, dot with remaining 2 T. margarine and stir lightly. Remove thyme and parsley sprigs and bay leaf.

Serve immediately.

GOURMET PEAS

2-3 SERVINGS

1 c. peas, fresh or frozen
a few scallions (2 T. minced onion is good, but not *as* good as scallions)
½ t. brown sugar
rounded ½ t. salt
¼ t. basil
¼ t. chervil or thyme
freshly ground pepper
butter or margarine
2-3 large outer lettuce leaves

Put peas into a dry saucepan. Tuck a few scallions among them (the flavour is more delicate than onions . . .)

Sprinkle the sugar, salt, pepper, & herbs over peas.

Dot with butter or margarine.

Cover with the lettuce leaves, cover pan tightly.

Start the cooking on low heat. Soon moisture from the lettuce and from the melting butter will filter down through the peas and will prevent scorching.

Cook until just tender. Remove the lettuce before serving the peas.

* One pound of fresh peas in the pod equals about one cup of hulled peas.
  The lettuce imparts a very delicate flavour and is well worth the effort.

GREEN BEANS IN MUSHROOM SAUCE

SERVES 4-6

1 lb. fresh green beans or 1 pkg. frozen green beans
1 T. minced onion
½ t. salt
½ t. sugar
pepper to taste
1 t. basil or summer savory
1 can cream of mushroom soup
¼ c. bread crumbs
¼ c. slivered almonds or cashews
¼ c. wine (OPTIONAL)
bean sprouts (OPTIONAL)

Cook beans (French cut them if you want) with onion, sugar, and pepper.

Do not add salt until cooking is half over— this helps to avoid toughening the beans.

Drain and add basil, mushroom soup, nuts, optional ingredients. Mix together and put in casserole dish.

Top with bread crumbs.

* Bake at 350° for about 20 minutes.

CREAMED KOHLRABI

SERVES 2 OR 3

For some reason, kohlrabi isn't very well known, and you may have to hunt around to find it. But it's really worth it. We buy it from a farm in New Hampshire. It grows very easily from seed and you can sometimes buy it at the supermarket in summer, so we're including this good recipe in case you can get ahold of some. Try it, and then turn a friend on to it!

4 small kohlrabis
1/4 c. butter
1/4 c. heavy cream

Remove and discard the stems and leaves; then peel the kohlrabis and cut them in small dice. Boil in 1 c. water 30-40 minutes until very tender when stuck with a knife point.

Drain any water that's left in the pan, then add the butter and stir around until all the pieces are coated, over medium heat.

Stir in the cream and let it get hot but not boiling. (about 3 min.)

Kohlrabi is good raw, too.

MUSHROOM PIE

SERVES 3 OR 4

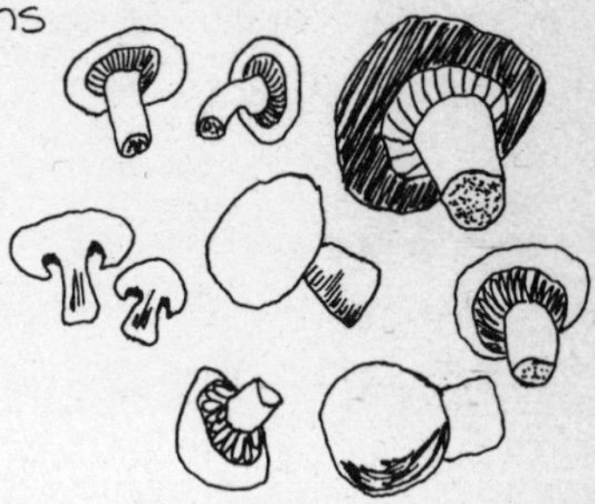

about 1 lb. fresh mushrooms
2 T. margarine
1/4 c. sour cream
1/4 t. salt
a couple grinds of pepper
1 T. flour
1/4 c. chopped parsley
1/2 c. grated swiss or cheddar cheese

Slice the mushrooms into 1/4" slices. Sauté in the margarine, stirring frequently until brown—in a couple minutes the juices will form.

Mix together the sour cream, salt, pepper, and flour and stir until smooth. Stir it in with the mushrooms and keep stirring until bubbly.

Spread in a smallish glass or ceramic pie plate and sprinkle cheese and parsley on top.

✿ Bake at 400° for 15 minutes, or until the cheese has melted and mushrooms are hot.

STUFFED MUSHROOM CAPS

4 SMALL SERVINGS

1 doz. large fresh mushrooms
1 T. margarine
1 c. Pepperidge Farm stuffing
1 ½ T. chopped chives
pinch of tarragon
pinch of basil
2 T. of cream, milk, melted margarine, sherry, red or white wine, or water — OR any combination equal to 2 T.
salt to taste

Wipe mushrooms lightly with a damp cloth if gritty. Break off stems at base, near gills.

Chop up stems and cook in a small saucepan with 1 T. margarine for about 2 minutes, stirring frequently.

Add about 1 c. stuffing and the chives, tarragon, and basil.

Add 2 T. liquid in whatever combination you prefer and mix well. Add salt, stir, and taste. More liquid may be added if mixture is terribly crumbly.

Brush the outsides of the mushroom caps with margarine, then fill the insides with the bread-crumb mixture.

Place stuffed side up in a shallow, greased pan.

Broil, checking frequently to prevent burning, about 5 minutes. Serve hot.

SOUR CREAM MUSHROOMS

SERVES 4 AS A VEGETABLE

1 lb. fresh mushrooms, sliced
½ c. minced onions
4 T. margarine
1 t. salt
¼ t. freshly ground black pepper
2 t. paprika
1 c. sour cream

Sauté the onions in the margarine for 5 min.

Add the sliced mushrooms and season with salt and pepper.

Stirring frequently, sauté over medium heat until the mushrooms are brown and most of the liquid has evaporated. (Mushrooms exude lots of liquid.)

Stir in the paprika and carefully add the sour cream, a little at a time, stirring until well blended.

Heat, stirring occasionally, but do not let the mixture boil (bubble).

* Serve on whole wheat toast, crackers, or even plain.

CARROT AND POTATO CURLS

SERVES 2

2 T. margarine
2 T. water
1 potato, peeled
2 carrots
1 small onion
Salt & pepper to taste

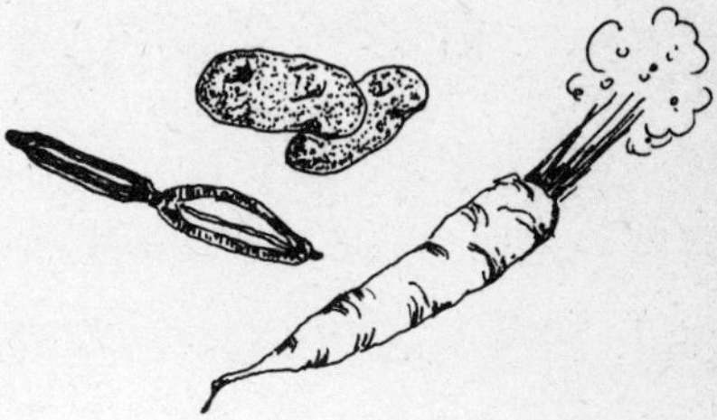

Melt margarine in a heavy skillet.
Slice onion thinly, sauté in skillet until soft.
Wash, dry, and chill carrots and potato.
With a vegetable peeler, peel the potato & carrots (the whole vegetable, not just the skin) directly into the skillet. Add water.
Turn up heat & stir constantly until the potato curls are cooked through.
Season to taste & serve immediately.

✲ The thinner the curls, the faster they will cook... If you don't like cooked potato skins, peel them off and use for stock.

HUTSPOT

SERVES 2 OR 3

2 medium potatoes
½ large onion
3-4 carrots
salt to taste
pepper to taste
margarine
milk

Peel chilled potatoes and cut into chunks.

Mince onion and put into a small saucepan along with the potato chunks and enough water to steam them in. Add ¼ t. salt. Cover tightly and simmer until very tender.

Wash, dry, and chop carrots. Steam in a small amount of water until tender enough to mash.

Mash potatoes and onions and carrots together. Press through a food mill if you want a very fine consistency.

Add warm milk, salt, and pepper, and butter or margarine to taste. Beat vigorously and correct seasonings. Serve warm.

CRISP POTATO WEDGES

These taste very much like French fries, only there's no frying involved. They're fat and chunky like English chips . . . but it's a Swedish recipe!

SERVES 2

3 medium potatoes
4 T. melted butter or margarine
salt
pepper

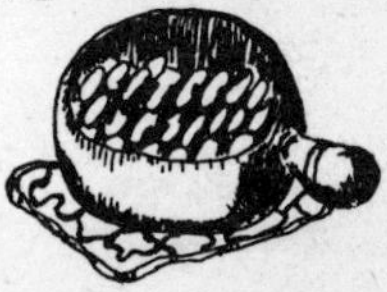

Peel potatoes and cut in lengthwise strips or wedges about ½ inch thick. Blanch the pieces by putting them in unsalted water to cover and boiling for about 3 minutes — this sets the color.

Drain and dry them with paper towels.

Butter a baking dish and stand them upright in a single layer. Dribble the melted butter over the wedges and sprinkle liberally with salt. (For a slightly different flavour, try using all or part fresh bacon fat in place of the melted butter.)

Bake uncovered at 450° for 30 minutes. Turn the wedges over once or twice during this time.

* Obviously, this recipe can be doubled or tripled or whatever.

LACE POTATOES

SERVES ABOUT 2

2 or 3 medium potatoes
½ small onion, minced fine
salt and pepper to taste
2 T. margarine
1 T. cooking or salad oil

Melt the margarine and oil in a heavy skillet. Add onion and sauté until soft.

Peel the potatoes and grate them coarsely into a bowl. Don't drain off the juice. Add salt and pepper and mix thoroughly.

Use about 2 T. of the potato mixture and flatten with a fork or spatula to form a small "pancake".

Fry about 4 minutes on each side or until crispy and gold and cooked through. Serve immediately.

SWEET POTATO SOUFFLÉ

SERVES 6

2 c. mashed sweet potatoes (2-3 whole potatoes)
½ c. hot milk
4 T. butter
dash of nutmeg
½ t. salt
1 t. powdered lemon rind
¼ c. brown sugar
4 egg yolks, beaten
4 egg whites, beaten stiff.

Add milk and butter to potatoes. Whip smooth (by hand or mixer). Add everything else but the egg whites and beat again.

Fold in the whites, VERY GENTLY, and turn into a buttered soufflé dish.

✿ Bake at 400° for 25-35 minutes until puffy and brown.

✿ This goes really well with the BAKED HAM SLICE (p. 56).

* Sweet potatoes have a very high vitamin A content.

SPROUTS – HOW AND WHAT

The why is easy — fresh sprouts are good, easy, inexpensive, and nutritious. Do it.

In Scott and Helen Nearing's book, *Living the Good Life*, they say, "A bean, pea, corn kernel or other seed is a whole food. Each contains a life germ, a complete source of nutriment. All seeds, including grains, contain protein, oil, vitamins, and other potent life-giving sources designed by nature to nourish the germ until the new plant gets down roots and sends up shoots which will enable it to secure nourishment on its own behalf. . . Whole, entire, raw seeds, with the protein of the germ, the fat in the oil, the starch in the kernel, and the minerals distributed through the protective covering, will provide a fairly rounded diet on which animal life can be sustained for a long time."

An important facet of good nutrition is eating all the nutriments *at the same time*. That's awfully hard to plan for in the usual American meal-planning way. The seeds (and sprouts) seem to be a good answer. In many parts of the country it's about the only way to get really fresh "vegetables" in winter.

There are a lot of things you can sprout, but if you havn't done it before, we recommend starting with mung beans or alfalfa seed because they taste so good you won't be discouraged when you sprout your first (and last) batch of something you don't like — like sunflower seeds.

Soak 1/4 c. mung beans in lukewarm water in a big jar overnight. The next morning some time, pour off all the water. (Save the water; it's supposed to contain wondrous nutriments, and when chilled in the refrigerator, it's very thirst-quenching.) Cover the jar with a towel and put it in a warm dark place (a cupboard or closet). Or, instead of the towel you can cover the jar with a small, sandwich-size baggie, with the corners cut off for ventilation. Yet another variation would be to use a large dark brown glass jar — this can be left out on the counter since it effectively cuts out too much light just as it is. Be sure to cover it with something, however, so all the moisture doesn't evaporate.

Twice a day fill the jar with warm water, just to rinse the beans. Then pour it all off, re-cover, and return to the cupboard. The point is to keep them warm and moist, but not wet. After 2-3 days, they'll be ready to eat. Your 1/4 c. beans will make about 4 cups of sprouts, 2-3 inches long. When they've sprouted enough, keep them in the refrigerator to keep them from growing too much more.

Alfalfa seeds are sprouted the same way except that they don't need to be soaked the first night and it only takes about 1 T. seeds to make 3-4 cups sprouts.

The last time you fill the jar with water you can scoop off the husks that float to the surface — but it isn't necessary.

You can eat sprouts raw, add to salads and bread dough, soups, eggs, and stewed tomatoes, or cook them as we do:

Fry 1 small chopped onion in 4 T. margarine until soft. Add about 2 c. sprouts and stir around for 5 minutes. Add 2 T. soy sauce. Eat.

* Some other sproutables (Be sure to get the UNTREATED kind):

soybeans	whole wheat berries
lentils	rye
garbanzos	oats
radish seeds	barley
kidney beans	peas - green
	peas - chick (good snacks

SUMMER SQUASH AND TOMATOES

SERVES 4

2 c. summer squash, sliced
3 T. margarine
1 onion, thinly sliced
1 large tomato, sliced
pepper
2 T. water
½ t. salt

Melt margarine in a covered skillet.

Slice and sauté the onion until golden.

Slice tomato, slice squash into ¼" slices — add to onions in skillet.

Add a couple grinds of pepper and the water — stir gently, cover tightly. Simmer until squash is tender, about 5 minutes. Shake pan occasionally to keep the vegetables from sticking.

Season with salt, and garnish with chopped parsley or chives if you want.

ZUCCHINI IN DILL SAUCE

SERVES 2

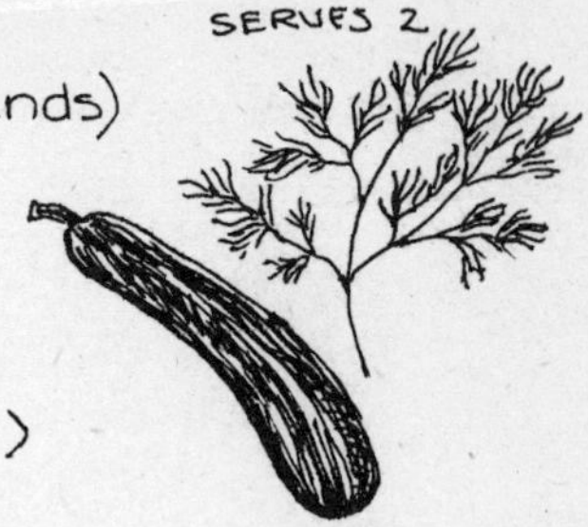

1 lb. zucchini (sliced in 1/4" rounds)
3 T. margarine
1/2 c. sour cream
1/4 t. sugar
1/2 t. vinegar (or lemon juice)
1 t. dill weed

Melt the margarine in a pan that has a cover. Add zucchini and stir-fry about 5 minutes until light brown.

Cover. Turn heat to low and simmer 10 minutes. Then stir in the sour cream and let it heat up about 2 minutes.*

Remove from heat and stir in the sugar, vinegar, and dill.

* Don't let it boil after you've added the sour cream or it will curdle. However, if it does curdle, don't worry. It still tastes all right — it just looks funny.

APPLESAUCE CAKE

1 c. brown sugar
1 ½ c. applesauce (15 oz.)
½ t. salt
1 t. cloves
1 t. cinnamon
1 t. nutmeg or ½ t. mace or 3/4 t. nutmeg & ¼ t. mace
2 t. soda
2 ½ c. flour — all-purpose or whole wheat
1 c. raisins or currants
chopped nuts — optional
¼ c. & 1 T. cooking oil

Mix together the applesauce and brown sugar.

Sift the dry ingredients together; salt, cloves, cinnamon, nutmeg, soda, and flour.

Add the oil to the sugar mixture, blending as thoroughly as you can. Then stir in the dry ingredients a little at a time.

Stir in the raisins (and nuts).

Pour into a greased and floured 9" square pan.

✿ Bake at 350° for about 45 minutes or until a cake tester comes out clean.

✱ If you don't happen to have enough applesauce, or if you just feel like it, use part canned pie apples. Thin too-thick applesauce with sweet fruit juice, like orange or apple.

BLACK-OUT CAKE

Cake: 1 pkg. Red Devil's Food Cake Mix
1 pint soft chocolate ice cream
1/2 c. water
3 eggs

Put everything in a bowl and beat 2 min.

Turn into a greased and floured 10" tube pan if you have one, or 2 8" cake pans.

* Bake at 350° — 25 minutes for 2 pans
45 minutes for 1 pan

Cool completely before you frost.

Fudge Frosting: 5 oz. unsweetened chocolate
1 stick margarine
1 box powdered sugar
1/2 c. evaporated milk
1 t. vanilla
6 crushed Pepperidge Farm Fudge Chip Cookies

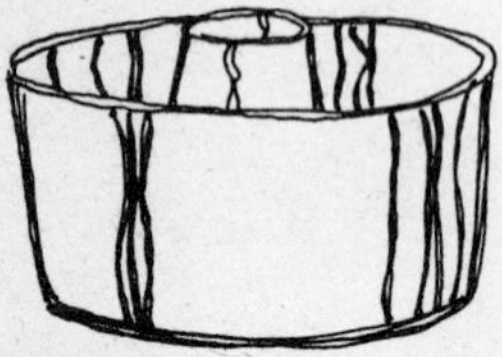

Melt butter and chocolate together over low heat. Remove from heat and beat in sugar & milk alternately until all the sugar is gone. Stir in vanilla.

It's the right consistency when it's just a little too thick to pour. Frost cake completely and cover with cookie crumbs.

If you have left-over frosting, add a little more evaporated milk for a super fudge sauce for ice cream. Keep it in the refrigerator. Heat it up in a double boiler (over water), use what you want, and re-store for future use — it keeps forever.

BLUEBERRY CAKE

1 egg, beaten
2/3 c. sugar
1 1/2 c. flour
2 t. baking powder
1/2 t. salt
1/3 c. milk
3 t. melted margarine
1 t. vanilla
1 c. fresh blueberries — frozen thawed or drained canned also work

Gradually add the sugar to the beaten egg, mixing thoroughly.

Sift the flour, baking powder, and salt and dredge the berries in the mixture, then set the berries aside.

Add the flour mixture to the egg mixture alternately with the milk.

Add the melted butter and the vanilla. Stir.

Carefully fold in the dredged berries.

Pour into a greased 8"x8" cake pan and sprinkle lightly with sugar.

Bake at 400° for about 40 minutes or until a toothpick comes out clean.

Serve warm...

CREAMY CHEESECAKE

PART 1 : GRAHAM CRACKER CRUST

1 ½ c. pulverized graham crackers
(3 crackers = approx. ½ cup)
½ c. sugar (or less, depending on taste)
½ c. melted margarine
1 t. cinnamon

Combine all ingredients well, press evenly into a pie pan with your fingers. Refrigerate while you prepare the filling.

PART II : CHEESECAKE FILLING

2 8-oz. pkgs. cream cheese, room temperature.
2 eggs
¾ c. sugar
1 t. vanilla

Put everything in a bowl and beat until smooth.
Pour into prepared, chilled graham cracker crust.
Bake at 375° for about 25 minutes. It is done when it begins to crack in the center, but it doesn't *have* to crack to be done. Center will still be slightly damp-looking.

PART III : SOUR CREAM TOPPING

1 pint sour cream
⅓ c. sugar
1 t. vanilla

Beat topping ingredients together for 5 min.

If you want, sprinkle a fine layer of cinnamon sugar over the baked cheesecake.

Spread the sour cream topping mixture (as much of it as will conveniently stay on top) over the cinnamon sugar layer.

Bake for 10 minutes at 350°.

Refrigerate at least 6 hours before serving.

* A tasty variation is to omit the sour cream topping and use instead a can of chilled prepared cherry pie filling. In this case you would also omit the cinnamon sugar layer and would not return it to the oven for the additional 10 minutes — just refrigerate.

* Don't buy ready-made graham cracker crusts. They are rarely, if ever, refrigerated in a market; they contain fats which can become rancid after a while when not refrigerated. Rancidity destroys vitamins A, E, K, and some B vitamins when it occurs in food, or even in the body or bloodstream.

DUTCH APPLE CAKE

packaged biscuit mix - recipe for coffee cake -
(you may need sugar, an egg, milk, or water, depending on the mix - we use the popular buttermilk baking mix kind)
2-3 apples
1/4 c. sugar
2 t. cinnamon
milk or cream
sugar
nutmeg

Prepare batter for coffee cake and spread in a greased, shallow baking dish.

Arrange a layer of peeled apple slices on the batter, tucking the thin edges into the batter.

Sprinkle a mixture of cinnamon (2 t.) and sugar (1/4 c.) over the apples.

✿ Bake at 350° until apples are tender.

At the table, after the individual portions have been served, pass around a small pitcher of milk or cream, the sugar bowl, and the nutmeg & grater. Best if served warm.

✿ This is old fashioned but quick. It has a sort of country kitchen flavour and aroma.

LOAM CAKE

1 ½ c. whole wheat flour
1 c. brown sugar-packed
3 T. cocoa
1 t. soda
½ t. salt
5 T. salad or cooking oil
1 T. vinegar
1 t. vanilla
1 c. cold water OR applesauce

Mix dry ingredients together or sift directly into an ungreased 8" cake pan.

Make 3 holes in the mixture.

Pour oil in one hole, vinegar in another, and vanilla in the third hole.

Pour cold water OR applesauce over all.

Stir with a fork until evenly blended, being sure to get the corners.

Bake at 350° for 35-40 minutes

Serve as is or with Maple Frosting (p.103).

MAPLE FROSTING

This makes enough to frost two 8" or 9" layers or a 13" x 9½" cake.

2 ¾ c. confectioner's sugar (sift if lumpy)
½ t. salt
1 egg
¼ c. maple syrup
½ c. shortening
2 t. vanilla

Mix together sugar, salt, and egg.
Blend in syrup.
Add shortening and vanilla. Mix until smooth.
Add more sugar to thicken, water to thin.

ORANGE CAKE

3 eggs, separated
1 T. strained orange juice
1 orange rind, grated
1 ½ c. sugar
⅛ t. salt
1½ t. baking powder
1 ½ c. flour
½ c. boiling water

Beat the egg yolks thoroughly. Add the orange juice and the sugar and beat for 10 minutes.

Add the salt, orange rind, water, and stiffly beaten egg whites.

Add the flour and baking powder and mix well.

Pour into a greased and floured 9" square pan. Bake at 350° for 30 minutes or until a toothpick comes out clean.

ORANGE FROSTING

1 ½ t. orange rind
¼ c. orange juice
salt to taste
6 T. butter or margarine
3 c. confectioner's sugar

combine all ingredients & beat until creamy smooth.

POPPY SEED CAKE

SERVES LOTS

about 2 ¼ oz. poppy seeds (a small jar or box)
1 c. milk
1 ½ c. sugar
2 c. flour
2 ½ t. baking powder
¼ t. salt
½ c. shortening
2 eggs
¼ - ½ t. vanilla extract

Soak the seeds in 1 c. milk for an hour.

Sift together the sugar, flour, baking powder, and salt. Add gradually to the seeds and milk along with the shortening and mix for 2 minutes until smooth. (This is the electric mixer method—if you're mixing by hand, cream together the sugar and shortening, add milk and seeds, then dry ingredients.)

Add vanilla and eggs and mix two more minutes.

Pour into a greased 10" square pan.

Bake at 350° for 45 minutes or until a toothpick comes out clean.

Although this is called a cake, it is really best when served warm with butter or margarine.

SUNDAY CAKE

1/3 c. softened margarine or butter
2/3 c. sugar
2 eggs, beaten singly
2/3 c. sifted flour
2 t. baking powder
1/4 t. salt
1/2 t. vanilla extract
1/4 t. almond extract

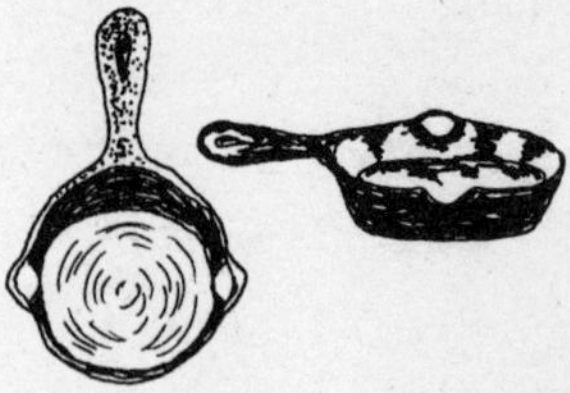

Cream together margarine and sugar.

Beat eggs singly; add to the creamed mixture, stirring each until thoroughly blended.

Sift together flour, baking powder, and salt. Add gradually to the sugar mixture; stir well.

Add the vanilla and almond extracts & stir.

Grease an 8 or 9" iron skillet and lightly dust with flour.

* Bake at 325° for 35 minutes.

Cool on a rack for 10 minutes before turning out on a plate.

Sprinkle with sifted confectioner's sugar and serve immediately.

BREAKFAST COOKIES

1 c. raisins
1 c. shredded coconut
1 c. Total, Kellog's K, Team, Product 19, etc.
1 c. quick oats
2 c. whole wheat flour
½ t. baking powder
½ t. soda
½ t. salt
3/4 c. shortening
3/4 c. brown sugar
2 eggs
1 t. vanilla

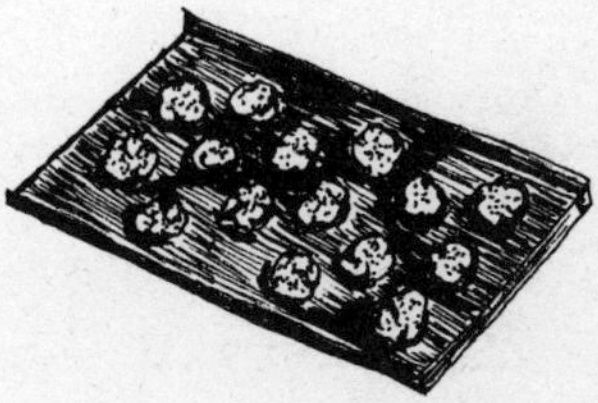

Combine raisins, coconut, cereal, oats, flour, baking powder, soda, and salt. Set aside.

Cream together shortening and sugar. Beat in eggs and vanilla.

Add dry ingredients, mixing with a spoon as well as you can, then mixing with your hands.

Form walnut-sized balls with hands and place on greased cookie sheet. Flatten with hand.

Bake at 375° for 10-12 minutes.

CHOCOLATE CHIP COOKIES

MAKES LOTS

2 1/4 c. flour
1 t. salt
1 t. baking soda
1 c. soft shortening
3/4 c. raw sugar
3/4 c. brown sugar
1/2 t. water
1 t. vanilla
2 eggs, well-beaten
2 c. semi-sweet chocolate bits (12 oz. package)
1 c. chopped nuts (opt.)

Sift together flour, salt, and soda.

Cream shortening and sugars together, add water and vanilla and beat until creamy.

Add beaten eggs, mix well.

Add flour mixture, a little at a time, mixing thoroughly. Stir in chocolate bits (and nuts).

Drop by teaspoonfuls onto a greased cookie sheet. They spread, so not too close together!

Bake at 375° for about 10 minutes.

GRAM'S OATMEAL COOKIES

1 c. packed brown sugar
1/3 c. salad or cooking oil — just roughly mix
1/2 t. salt

Add: 1/2 t. baking soda dissolved in
1/4 c. water

Stir until brown sugar is dissolved.

Add: 1 c. oats
1/2 t. vanilla
flour to stiffen

Mix thoroughly.

Roll and press dough as thin as possible on a greased cookie sheet. Use both a rolling pin and your fingers.

Score with a knife into squares or oblongs about 3" x 3".

Bake in a preheated 350° oven, about 5 minutes.

While cookies are still warm, remove them from the cookie sheet with a broad spatula by gently breaking them along the scored lines. If they cool too quickly for easy removal, pop them back into the oven to warm them.

GRANOLA COOKIES

MAKES 3 DOZEN

Cream together:

- 1/2 c. shortening
- 1/2 c. white sugar
- 1/4 c. brown sugar
- 1 egg

Mix together:

- 1 cup flour
- 1/2 t. baking soda
- 3/4 t. cinnamon

Add it to the creamed mixture.
Then stir in:

- 3/4 c. crunchy granola OR VIGEROLA
- 1/4 c. chopped nuts
- 1 t. vanilla

Chill the dough for 1 hour.*
Drop by the teaspoonful on a greased cookie sheet.
Bake at 350° for 8 minutes.

* This is important unless you want one giant cookie...

Hot Chicken Salad

8 ch breasts

French dressing

1 c celery

1 c mayonaise

1 lb jar Cheese Whiz

1 c t fried onions

350 $\frac{1}{2}$ hr or longer

Marinate cooked chicken in french dressing over night then cook all in 350 oven $\frac{1}{2}$ hr or longer

Serve with rice & Salad

PEANUT BUTTER COOKIES

MAKES ABOUT 4 DOZEN

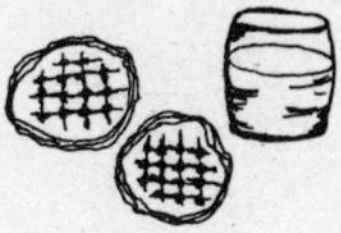

1 ½ c. flour
1 t. soda
dash salt
½ c. shortening
1 c. packed brown sugar
1 beaten egg
½ c. peanut butter
½ t. vanilla
3 T. sesame seeds (opt.)

Mix or sift flour, soda, and salt together. Set aside.

Cream shortening and sugar together. Add beaten egg, mix well, then add peanut butter, vanilla (and sesame seeds). Mix thoroughly.

Add flour mixture, a little at a time, blending well. Mixture will be quite stiff.

Roll the dough into walnut-size balls and place on an ungreased cookie sheet. Press them flat with a fork making a cross-hatch pattern.

✲ Bake at 375° for about 10 minutes.

CRYSTALLIZED MINT LEAVES

2 lbs. mint leaves
5 c. sugar
2 c. water
a pinch of cream of tartar

Remove mint leaves from stalks, wash in cold water, spread on white paper to dry. Don't use paper towels — they leave lint on the leaves. Something like typing or shelf paper works best.

Place 4 cups sugar together with water into a saucepan and dissolve thoroughly, stirring with a candy thermometer. When dissolved, add cream of tartar and cook until syrup forms a soft ball when tested in cold water, or to 236°.

Remove pan from heat and add mint leaves, putting them a few at a time carefully into the syrup and pressing them down under the syrup.

Return to heat and allow to boil up once, then put the pan immediately into the refrigerator to cool it down.

The following day, warm syrup in order to soften it, then remove leaves and drain on a wire rack. Add the remaining cup of sugar to the syrup in the pan and cook to soft ball stage, 236°.

Drop mint leaves back in, set aside overnight.

The third day, drain again. Bring syrup to the boiling point. Add the mint. Remove from heat and stir gently until syrup begins to grain, then pour onto sheets of paper. Shake and separate the leaves.

When the leaves are dry, pick them from the sugar.

* Although the recipe calls for 2 lbs. of mint leaves, we have made it successfully with far less than that, using the same amount of syrup.

PEANUT CLUSTERS

1 6 oz. bag semi-sweet chocolate bits
1 jar salted, dry-roasted peanuts

Melt chocolate bits over low heat in a double boiler or a heavy saucepan, stirring until completely melted.

Remove from heat and stir in as many peanuts as you want.

Drop by teaspoonfuls onto waxed paper.

Place on a level surface in the refrigerator until hard (it doesn't take long).

* These are a cinch to make and easy to eat, too!

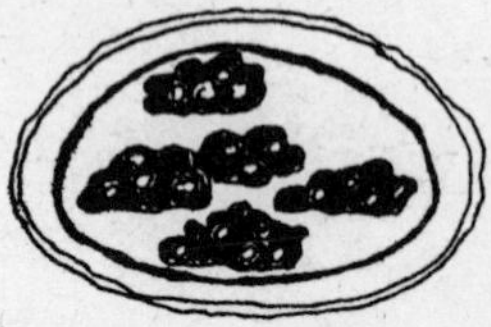

BLONDE BROWNIES

1/4 c. cooking oil
1 c. brown sugar
1 egg
3/4 c. flour
1 t. baking powder
1/2 t. salt
1/2 t. vanilla
1/2 c. chopped nuts

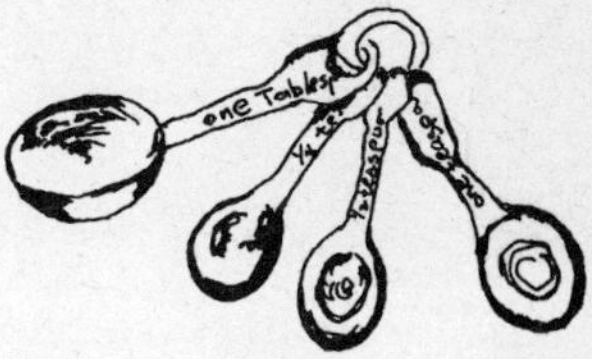

Stir the brown sugar and oil together.
Add the egg and stir thoroughly.
Sift together the flour, baking powder, and salt and add to the sugar mixture. Blend well. Add the vanilla and the nuts.
Bake at 350° in a greased 8" square pan for about 25 minutes.

* These taste best if they're slightly chewy. Don't overcook or they'll get hard.

CHEWY-FUDGE BROWNIES

5 squares unsweetened chocolate
1 stick margarine
½ c. shortening
4 eggs
¼ t. salt
2 c. sugar
1 T. vanilla
1 c. flour

Melt together in a saucepan over low heat:
chocolate
margarine
shortening

Beat eggs with salt & sugar. Add chocolate mixture and vanilla.

Add flour and beat smooth.

✿ Pour into a greased and floured 9" square pan and bake at 325° for 50 minutes.

These are really fine plain, but for a special treat frost with Chocolate Glaze (p.120).

DATE BARS

MAKES ABOUT 30

3 c. ground dates (or about 1 lb. pitted dates)
1/3 c. brown sugar
1 c. orange juice

This is the filling mixture — mix everything together in a saucepan. Cook over low heat, stirring constantly, until mixture thickens. Set aside to cool.

For the crust . . .
3/4 c. soft margarine
3/4 c. brown sugar
1 1/4 c. flour
1/4 c. wheat germ
1 t. baking powder
1/2 t. salt
1 3/4 c. rolled oats

Mix together margarine and brown sugar.

Mix together (or sift) flour, baking powder, and salt, stir in wheat germ. Stir into the sugar mixture along with the oats. Mix well.

Place half the mixture into a greased 9x13 baking pan. Press with hands to cover bottom of pan. Spread cooled filling to within 1/4" of edges. Cover with rest of mixture, pat lightly.

Bake at 400° for 25-30 minutes until light brown. Cut in squares while warm.

QUICK DONUTS

(ALSO CHEAP)

1 tube refrigerated buttermilk biscuits (the regular kind —not the new FLAKY)

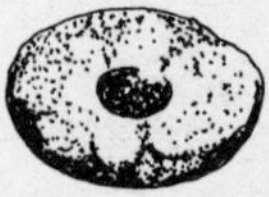

Remove biscuits from tube.

Punch a small hole in the center of each.

Fry one or two at a time in 1" of hot fat (crisco or oil) until golden — about 1-2 min. each. Heat the fat over medium or it will get too hot too fast.

CHOCOLATE GLAZE

about 3/4 cup

Melt together over low heat (while you're making the donuts):
- 1 T. margarine
- 1 square unsweetened chocolate
- 2 T. hot water
- 1 T. corn syrup (not absolutely essential)

When it's all melted together, remove from heat and stir in just enough powdered sugar to make it bittersweet but still pourable.

Spoon over hot donuts.

PAN BANANAS

SERVES 4

3 T. butter
4 bananas
4 T. brown sugar
½ t. cinnamon
¼ c. orange juice

Melt butter in a frying pan. When it's bubbly, add bananas, split lengthwise. Sprinkle with brown sugar and cinnamon and sauté until lightly browned on both sides. Pour in juice and swirl it around until heated.

Tastes good with:

WHITE CUSTARD CREAM

2 c. heavy cream
3 T. sugar
4 egg whites
1 egg yolk
1 ½ t. vanilla

Scald 1 cup of the cream over medium heat. Stir in the sugar. Remove from heat.

Beat the whites until thick and frothy, then beat in the rest of the cream and the yolk. Continue to beat at high speed about 2 minutes more.

Stir a little of the hot cream into the cold cream, then pour all of the cold cream into the pan and cook, stirring constantly, over medium heat until thickened (about 5 minutes).

Add vanilla, cool, and pour into a bowl. Cover and store in the refrigerator.

* About the egg whites:

Whenever you have a recipe that calls for just yolks, pour the leftover whites in an ice cube tray (1 per cube-hole) and freeze. When you have 4 whites, make White Custard Cream...

INDIAN PUDDING

SERVES 8

1 qt. milk (4 c.)
1/3 c. corn meal
3/4 c. molasses
1/4 c. butter or margarine
1 t. salt
1 t. ginger
1/4 t. nutmeg
1/2 t. cinnamon
3 T. brown sugar
1 well-beaten egg

Boil milk in top of double boiler over direct heat.

Stir in corn meal. Place over boiling water and cook for about 15 minutes until mixture begins to thicken. Stir frequently.

Stir in molasses – cook 5 more minutes.

Remove from heat & stir in remaining ingredients.

Pour into a buttered baking dish.

* Bake at 325° for 1½-2 hours, or until a silver knife inserted in center comes out clean.

Serve warm with cream, vanilla ice cream, or Hard Sauce.

OZARK PUDDING

- 3/4 c. brown sugar
- 4 T. margarine
- 2 beaten eggs
- 2/3 c. flour
- 1/2 t. salt
- 1 t. cinnamon
- 1/2 t. nutmeg
- 1/3 c. wheat germ
- 1 t. vanilla
- 1/2 c. chopped walnuts
- 2 c. peeled, cored, diced apples (about 2 large apples)

Cream brown sugar and margarine together. Stir in beaten eggs.

Sift dry ingredients together (except for wheat germ) and add to sugar mixture. Stir in wheat germ.

Add vanilla, walnuts, and apples. Blend thoroughly.

Bake in a greased pie plate for 35-40 minutes at 350°.

Serve warm with whipped cream, milk, vanilla ice cream, or whatever you want.

FRESH FRUIT CUP

1-2 red-skinned apples, cored, cubed, but not peeled
1-2 bananas, peeled and sliced in rounds
1-2 oranges, sectioned, and some of the juice
1-2 grapefruits, sectioned, and some of the juice
fresh melon balls if available (cantaloupe, watermelon, Muskmelon, honeydew, Persian melon, etc.)
grapes - green or Concord - sliced in half, seeds removed (be sure to check for union stamp on box)
pomegranate (opt.) - squeeze seed juice for color
mango (opt.)
guava (opt.)
½ t. vanilla extract (approx.)
brown sugar (opt.)
crystallized mint leaves (opt.) - make a nice garnish

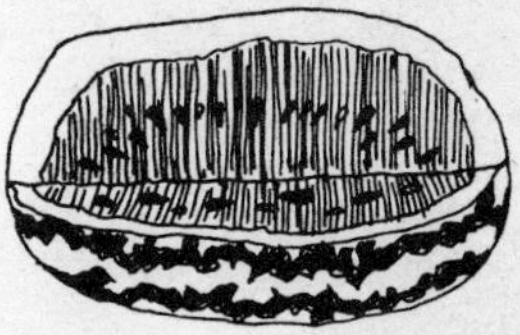

Combine fruits in a large bowl, using whatever combination you want.

Add ½-1 t. vanilla and stir lightly - this brings out the natural sugars.

A light sprinkling of brown sugar can be added if you prefer it sweeter. Or how about honey?

Pomegranate seeds squeezed over the fruit cup make a nice pink color; mint leaves are an attractive garnish and add subtle flavour.

PRUNE WHIP

If you, too, are an avid connoisseur of baby food, you should definitely try this.

SERVES ABOUT 3

2 eggs
3 T. sugar
3 jars baby food prunes
squirt of lemon

Beat the eggs until light and fluffy. Add the sugar and stir thoroughly. Add the prunes and lemon juice and stir. Adjust to suit your taste.

BRIGHT RED-FRUIT PUDDING

MAKES ABOUT 6

2 10 oz. pkgs. frozen raspberries, thawed
2 10 oz. pkgs. frozen strawberries, thawed
1/3 c. cornstarch
1/2 c. orange juice (or water—but juice is better)
1 T. lemon juice

Mix berries together in a saucepan. Bring to a boil over high heat, stirring constantly.

Add orange juice (or water) to cornstarch—then stir it into the fruit.

Bring back to a boil and cook 3 minutes, stirring constantly.

Remove from heat. Stir in the lemon juice.

Pour into bowls. Chill.

Serve with sweet whipped cream.

This is a good thing to make in the summer because when fresh fruit is available, frozen fruit prices drop.

KREM

MAKES 4

This Swedish pudding is similar to Bright Red-Fruit Pudding (p. 127) and is made the same way.

2 c. grape juice
3 T. sugar
3 T. cornstarch
3 T. water
1 t. lemon juice

Mix grape juice and sugar together in a saucepan. Bring to a boil over high heat, stirring constantly.

Mix the cornstarch with the water, then stir it into the grape juice. Bring up to a boil again and cook 3 minutes, stirring constantly.

Remove from heat, stir in lemon juice.

Pour into bowls. Chill.

Serve with whipped cream.

QUICK STRAWBERRY OR RASPBERRY MOUSSE

SERVES 4-6

1 c. sour cream
1 8 oz. box frozen strawberries (or raspberries), thoroughly thawed
½ c. sugar
1 ½ t. vanilla
pinch salt

Let berries thaw completely. Do not drain.
Combine all ingredients and beat well.
Pour into an ice cube tray.
Freeze.

This can be made 2 or 3 days ahead of time. Its pink color is festive and can be garnished with a few fresh berries in season. Good with coffee, and pass the cashews.

CHOCOLATE FUDGE PUDDING

MAKES 4 SERVINGS

2/3 c. chocolate chips
1 c. coffee cream (half & half)
3 T. sugar
1 whole egg & 2 yolks*
1 T. vanilla (or 1/2 vanilla, 1/2 almond extract)

Melt the chips in a small pan over low heat.
Remove from heat, and stir in sugar & cream.
Beat the eggs with a fork and pour slowly into the chocolate mixture, beating while you pour.
Stir in vanilla.
Pour into 4 1/2-cup custard cups and put the cups into a flat pan filled with hot water. (The water should come about half way up the cups.)
*Bake at 350° for about 20 minutes. The tops will be puffed into little domes when it's done.
Chill. Serve with sweetened whipped cream.

* If you don't eat it within 2 days, it will turn into candy—and it tastes incredibly good.

* Ah! Some left over whites to freeze for White Custard Cream! (p. 121)

BLENDER CHOCOLATE PUDDING

SERVES 3

1 c. chocolate chips
1 c. scalded coffee cream
1 egg yolk
1 t. vanilla
½ t. cinnamon

Put everything in the blender and whirl at highest speed until you can't hear the chips bouncing around (about 1 minute).

Pour into 3 small dishes and chill 3 hours.

* You can freeze leftover egg whites . . .

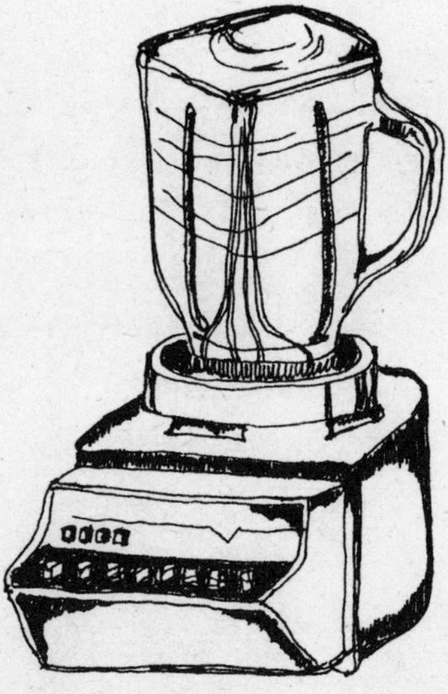

CHOCOLATE SOUFFLÉ

SERVES 6

This is not your average chocolate soufflé — it's easy to do and <u>always</u> rises right on cue.

1 small pkg. chocolate tapioca mix
6 eggs

Make the tapioca according to package directions. Then, while it's cooling, separate the eggs into 2 bowls.

Beat the whites until very stiff (TO TEST: turn the bowl upside down - if all the whites stay in place, they're ready.)

Then beat the yolks into the chocolate mixture.

Fold the stiff whites into the chocolate mixture VERY GENTLY.

* Pour into an ungreased 2 qt. casserole or soufflé dish. Bake 15-20 minutes at 425°.

Sprinkle with confectioner's sugar just before serving.

* This makes a crusty soufflé with a creamy filling. If you prefer it cakey all the way through, bake instead at 350° for 30 minutes.

MOCHA SOUFFLÉ

SERVES 6

3 T. margarine
3 T. flour
¼ c. strong coffee (¼ c. hot water, 1 T. instant coffee)
½ c. milk
3 heaping T. cocoa
⅓ c. whipping cream
4 eggs, separated
¼ t. salt
½ t. vanilla
⅓ c. sugar

Melt margarine in saucepan, gradually stir in flour, coffee, milk, cocoa, and cream. Cook until smooth and thick, stirring constantly. Set aside.

Beat together egg yolks, salt, vanilla, and sugar. Gradually add to first mixture, stirring thoroughly until blended. Return to heat and cook over low, stirring, until the egg yolks have begun to thicken. Remove from heat and let cool completely.

Fold in stiffly beaten egg whites.

Butter a 7" straight-sided soufflé type dish, dust with sugar, pour in batter. Set dish in a pan of hot water.

Bake at 350° for 35 minutes.

Serve immediately with sweetened whipped cream. Top with a few sprinkles of cinnamon.

CHEESE-ONION BREAD

MAKES 2 LOAVES

2 pkgs. yeast
1 1/4 c. hot water
1 c. sour cream
1 envelope onion soup mix
1/2 c. grated Swiss cheese (opt.)
1/4 t. baking soda
2 T. sugar
2 T. butter
2 eggs
6-7 c. all-purpose flour
Sesame seeds

Mix yeast with 2 c. of the flour and all the rest of the dry stuff (except seeds).

Add sour cream and hot water and beat for 2 minutes.

Add eggs and beat some more.

Stir in rest of flour, 1 cup at a time, until dough is stiff.

Knead about 10 minutes. Place in a greased bowl, cover, and let rise until double in bulk (about 1-1 1/2 hours).

Punch down and divide in half. Divide one half of the dough into thirds.

Roll each third into a rope about 12" long.

Braid the 3 ropes together tucking the ends under.

Repeat with the other half of dough.

Place the 2 braids next to each other on a greased cookie sheet (or in 2 loaf pans).

Let rise again about 45 min. - 1 hour.

Brush with beaten egg and sprinkle with sesame seeds.

Bake at 350° for 45 minutes.

VEGETABLE BREAD

MAKES 1 LOAF

1 c. grated carrots
½ c. tomato juice
1 small grated onion
2 T. dry parsley OR ¼ c. fresh
1 egg
½ c. grated cheddar cheese
2 T. oil
2 T. sugar
1 ½ t. salt
¼ c. warm water
1 pkg. dry yeast
3 c. flour

Soften the yeast in the water.

Mix everything else together well and stir in the yeast/water mixture. Work in with your hands about ¾ c. more flour. Turn dough onto floured counter and knead until smooth (about 10 min.).

Put into a greased bowl, cover, and let rise in a warm place until doubled in bulk (1-1½ hr.).

Punch down and shape into a loaf. Put into a greased loaf pan. Cover and let rise again for 45 minutes.

Bake at 375° for 1 hour.

GREAT AUNT EDA'S SWEDISH RYE BREAD

MAKES 1 LOAF

1 yeast cake
½ c. luke-warm water
2 c. all-purpose flour
2 c. rye flour
¼ t. salt
2 T. melted shortening —½ butter, ½ margarine
⅓ c. sugar
⅓ c. molasses

In a large bowl, dissolve the yeast cake in the luke-warm water.

Stir in the melted shortening, sugar, and molasses.

Sift together the two kinds of flour & the salt. Add to the yeast mixture, stirring and beating until blended. Additional luke-warm water will be needed — here you will have to use your own judgement, perhaps about ½ of a cup. If the dough seems too soft and sticky to handle, add a little more flour.

Knead lightly, cover, put in a warm place, and let rise until almost double.*

Stir down, shape into a loaf, and place in a lightly greased loaf pan. Let rise again until

* Rye bread takes longer to rise than other breads and it need not quite double in bulk.

almost double.

* Bake for about 1 hour at 300°.

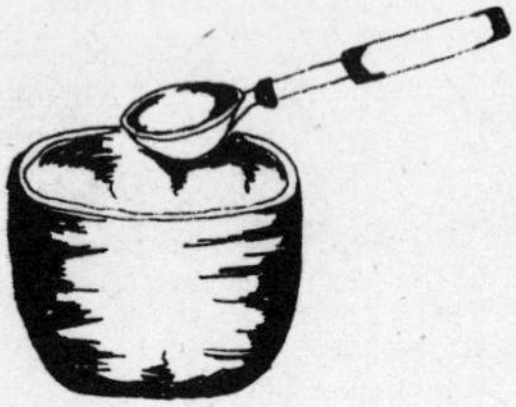

2 loaves.

Place in 2 large, lightly greased bread pans, cover with a damp cloth, and let rise a warm place until almost doubled in bulk (about 50 minutes).

Bake at 350° for about 1 hour. When done, loaves should sound hollow when tapped on the bottom or thumped on the side.

* SUNFLOWER BREAD makes fantastic toast.

APPLEWHEAT BREAD

MAKES 2 LOAVES

1 pkg. dry yeast
1/4 c. brown sugar
2 t. salt
1 c. flour
1 grated apple
1 1/4 c. hot water *
1 T. oil
1/2 c. applesauce
1/2 c. cooked oatmeal
about 4 c. whole wheat flour

Mix together in a large bowl: yeast, sugar, salt, and flour.

Mix together in a small bowl: apple, water, oil, applesauce, and oatmeal.

Add the wet mix to the dry mix and beat for 2 minutes (by hand or mixer).

Then stir in enough whole wheat flour to make a fairly stiff dough. Turn onto a floured counter and knead dough 10-12 minutes until smooth but not sticky.

(cont'd. next page)

* Preferably water in which potatoes or other vegetables have been cooked. The water you soaked your sprouts in is good for times like this.

Place in a greased bowl, cover, and let rise until double (about 1½ hours).

Punch down, re-cover, and let rise 1 hour.

Punch down and divide the dough in two.

Shape each half into a loaf and put into 2 well-greased loaf pans.

Cover and let rise 45 minutes.

Bake at 350° for 1 hour.

OATMEAL MUFFINS

MAKES ABOUT 12

1 c. cooked oatmeal
½ c. milk
¼ c. honey
1 beaten egg
2 c. flour
3 ½ T. baking powder
1 t. salt
3 T. cooking oil
½ c. raisins (opt.)

Mix together oatmeal and milk.

Add honey and beaten egg.

Sift dry ingredients and add to oatmeal, mixing thoroughly.

Add oil, blend thoroughly, stir in raisins.

Bake in greased muffin tins at 400° about half an hour or until a toothpick comes out clean.

WHOLE WHEAT MUFFINS

MAKES ABOUT A DOZEN

1 1/4 c. whole wheat flour
3/4 c. all-purpose flour
2 T. soy flour (opt.)
1 t. salt
2 1/2 t. baking powder

Mix or sift together in a bowl.
In another bowl put—

1 beaten egg
1 c. milk (or yogurt...)
4 T. melted butter or cooking oil
3 T. honey (or 2 T. molasses)

Mix wet ingredients thoroughly. Then stir into the dry ingredients—use a fork and work quickly, stirring just until blended. The batter should be somewhat lumpy.*

Fill greased muffin tins 2/3 full.
Bake at 400° for about 25 minutes.

* Too much stirring causes the gluten in the flour to toughen the dough.

WHOLE WHEAT ONION BUNS

MAKES ABOUT 8 BUNS

1 ½ T. margarine (that is, 1 T. & 1½ t.)
½ c. minced onion
1 ½ c. all-purpose flour
1 ½ c. whole wheat flour
1 ½ T. brown sugar
¾ t. salt
1 pkg. yeast
1 c. hot water

In a frying pan, melt margarine. Add the minced onion and sauté until golden, about 5 min.

In a large bowl mix together ½ c. regular flour, ½ c. whole wheat flour, brown sugar, salt, and yeast.

Reserve about 2 T. of the onion/butter mixture and stir the rest into the flour mixture. Pour in the hot water and blend well.

Stir in the rest of the flour (1 c. of each) and mix together to make a soft dough.

Turn dough onto a well-floured surface and knead until smooth & elastic, about 5 min. Add more whole wheat flour as needed to prevent sticking.

Place in a greased bowl, turning dough over to grease top. Cover and let rise in a warm place until doubled in bulk, about 1 hour.

Punch down & divide into 8 equal pieces.

Roll each piece into a ball and place about 4" apart on a well-greased baking sheet.

Flatten each ball into a 4" circle as well as you can.

Cover with a damp cloth & let rise in a warm place until almost doubled in bulk, about 50 min.

Spread about 1/4 t. of the onion/butter mixture on the top of each bun.

* Bake at 375° for about 25 minutes or until brown.

* These are especially good for Wilkieburgers (p. 62).

CHAPATIS
(INDIAN BREAD WAFERS)

1 DOZEN 5" BREADS

2 c. whole wheat flour
3 T. clarified butter
½-1 c. water

To make clarified butter, melt ½ stick (4 T.) butter in a small pan over low heat. When it's completely melted, remove from heat and let stand a few minutes while the sediment settles to the bottom. Skim the butter fat from the top & set aside—this is clarified butter.

To make the chapatis, combine flour and clarified butter. Blend in ¼ c. water. Add up to ¾ c. more water, 1 T. at a time, stirring well after each addition. Don't add any more water than is absolutely necessary to form a firm ball of dough.

Knead on a lightly floured board until smooth and elastic—about 8 minutes. Place in a bowl, cover with a damp cloth, and let rest 30 minutes.

Pinch off about 2 T. dough at a time, shape into a ball, and roll flat to about 5" in diameter. Heat a seasoned 10" iron griddle or a non-stick kind—do not grease the surface. When a drop of water sputters, add 1 chapati, moving it around constantly with your fingers or else

WHOLE WHEAT BANANA BREAD

1 LOAF

1 1/4 c. mashed bananas (about 2 bananas)
1/4 c. plain yogurt
3/4 c. brown sugar
1/2 stick margarine (1/4
1 egg
1 1/2 c. whole wheat flour
1 t. soda
1 t. salt.

Mix yogurt with mashed bananas.

In a large bowl, cream margarine and sugar together, then add the egg. Stir thoroughly.

In another bowl (or on a piece of paper) mix the dry ingredients together. Add alternately with the banana mixture to the butter and sugar mixture. Stir until combined.

Pour into a greased 9x5 loaf pan.

✿ Bake at 350° for about 1 hour or until a toothpick comes out clean.

Cool 15 minutes in the pan, then remove.

✿ This keeps for ages if it's well wrapped.

BANANA BRAN BREAD

MAKES 3 LOAVES

3/4 c. soft margarine
1 1/2 c. brown sugar
3 eggs
1/4 c. orange juice
2 c. whole OR flaked bran
3 c. mashed bananas
3 c. flour
4 t. baking powder
1 t. salt
1 t. baking soda

Cream margarine with sugar and eggs until fluffy, then stir in the bran.

Mix bananas with juice.

Mix together flour, baking powder, soda, and salt. Add this mixture to the creamed stuff alternately with the banana mixture.

Pour into 3 greased & floured loaf pans.

✽ Bake at 350° for 1 hour.

✽ This freezes well in case you can't eat all 3 right away.

PUMPKIN BREAD

MAKES 1 LOAF

1 1/3 c. sugar
1/3 c. shortening
2 eggs
1 c. pumpkin purée
1/3 c. water
1 2/3 c. flour—whole wheat
1/4 t. baking powder
1 t. baking soda
1/2 t. cinnamon
1/2 t. cloves
3/4 t. salt
1/3 c. chopped nuts

Cream together the sugar and shortening.

Add the eggs, pumpkin, and water and mix well.

Sift together all the dry ingredients and add gradually to the pumpkin mixture, blending thoroughly.

Stir in the chopped nuts.

Pour into a greased loaf pan (about 9¾" x 5½").

* Bake at 325° about 70 minutes. Toothpick should come out clean.

* This keeps well for several days if wrapped well.

APRICOT BREAD

MAKES 1 LOAF

½ c. dried apricots
1 large orange
2 T. margarine
1 c. sugar
1 t. almond extract
1 egg
2 c. flour
2 t. baking powder
½ t. baking soda
¼ t. salt
½ c. chopped nuts (if you want)

Soak the apricots in hot water ½ hour.

Squeeze orange juice into a 1 cup measure and add enough apricot water to make 1 cup.

Drain the apricots and chop in little pieces.

Mix together margarine, sugar, extract, and beat until really creamy. Mix in the apricots and nuts.

Mix together the flour, baking powder, soda, salt, and add to apricot mixture alternately with juice/water.

Pour into greased and floured loaf pan.

* Bake at 350° for 50-60 minutes.

* The almond extract really makes a difference so don't leave it out. You won't have any

trouble using up the rest of the bottle. Use a little in whipped cream or chocolate cake — it makes things richer-tasting!

CRANBERRY-ORANGE BREAD

MAKES 1 LOAF

This bears absolutely no resemblance to the heavy, soggy cranberry bread made with milk.

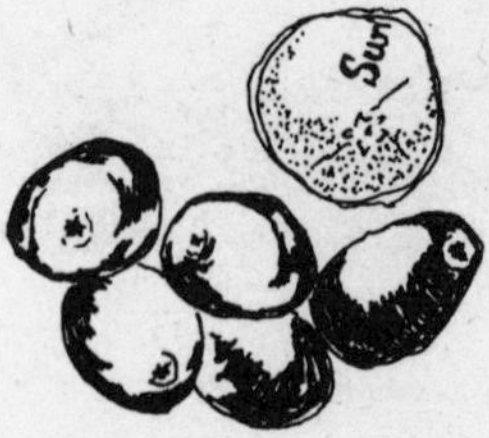

- 1/4 c. butter
- 1 c. sugar
- 1 egg
- 2 c. flour
- 1 t. baking soda
- 1/2 t. salt
- 1 c. orange juice (fresh is best)
- 1 c. chopped cranberries
- 1/2 c. chopped walnuts (optional)

Mix together: flour, soda, salt, and sugar.

Beat the egg and add to the orange juice, then pour into flour mixture. Stir just enough to mix — do not beat.

Add cranberries and nuts.

Turn into a greased and floured loaf pan.

Bake for 1 hour at 350°.

* Wondering what to do with the rest of the cranberries? Make Cranberry-Orange Sauce (p.165)

HONEY-CINNAMON BREAD

MAKES 1 LOAF

1 ½ c. sugar
1 ½ T. soft margarine
3 c. flour
1 c. honey
1 ½ t. cinnamon
1 t. baking soda
¼ t. mace (or nutmeg if you have an understandable aversion to mace)
1 c. milk

Blend the sugar and butter.

Stir in flour, honey, cinnamon, soda, and mace.

Then add milk and beat just until it's all mixed together.

✿ Turn into a greased loaf pan and bake at 400° for 35-40 minutes.

✿ This is good plain, but it's better with Apple Butter.

HONEY BUTTER

½ lb. butter
1 c. honey

Whip butter until fluffy.
Add honey gradually, and continue beating until very light.
Store in the refrigerator.

MAPLE BUTTER

½ lb. butter
1 c. maple syrup
¼ t. maple flavoring

Make the same as Honey Butter.

APPLE BUTTER

MAKES ABOUT 4 PINTS

Wash and remove the stems from 5 lbs. tart apples, then cut in slices. (The peels and seeds will be removed when you sieve so don't bother now.) Put the slices in a large kettle and pour in just enough cider (or grape juice) to cover the apples. Bring to a boil and simmer until apples are mushy — about 20 minutes.

Remove from heat and push apples through a sieve.

Then add to the pulp: 2 lbs. brown sugar
1 t. cinnamon
1 t. nutmeg
1 t. cloves

Stir it all together to dissolve the sugar, then return to heat and bring to a boil. Turn the heat to low, put an asbestos pad under the pot and simmer about 2 ½ hours, stirring occasionally, until very thick. It doesn't need much attention, but don't forget to stir it (about once every 20 min. is enough) or it will scorch.

If you're going to eat it within a couple of weeks, you don't have to seal the jars — just keep it in the refrigerator.
Otherwise: spoon into hot sterile jars leaving about ¼" space at the top. Seal

with a thin layer of melted paraffin, and when that has set, pour on another thin layer. Cover, label, and store in a cool, dark place.

PUMPKIN BUTTER

MAKES ABOUT 4 PINTS

6 lbs. pumpkin (2 small pumpkins)
about 3 c. brown sugar
1 T. lemon juice
1 c. finely chopped walnuts
2 t. cinnamon
½ t. nutmeg
½ t. cloves

Cut pumpkins in half. Remove seeds (save for Toasted Seeds, p. 1) and stringy stuff. Cut in chunks and remove rind. Boil the pieces in a covered pot with water just to cover for about 40 minutes, until mushy.

Drain off all excess water and push pumpkin through a sieve. Measure the pulp — there should be about 6 cups — and put it back into the pan, with ½ as much sugar. Add the lemon juice, nuts, and spices.

Cook on an asbestos pad over low heat until very thick, stirring occasionally.

TO TEST: Pour a Tablespoon of hot pumpkin butter on a cold plate — if no rim of liquid forms around the edge of the butter, it's ready. It will take about 3 hours of cooking to reach the right consistency.

PROCESS THE SAME AS APPLE BUTTER (p. 159).

SUN-COOKED STRAWBERRIES

4 c. (1 qt.) fresh strawberries
3-4 c. sugar
1 T. lemon juice (optional)

Clean and hull berries. Put into a large pan along with sugar (and lemon juice). DO NOT ADD ANY WATER. Stir gently with a wooden spoon, then let stand about 15 minutes or until some of the sugar has dissolved.

Cook over very low heat until all of the sugar has dissolved. Don't stir with a spoon—just shake the pan to prevent the berries from sticking or burning. When the mixture begins to boil, increase heat slightly and boil 10 minutes.

Remove from stove and pour into a shallow pan — a glass one is best. Skim off the foam when the berries have settled. Cover the pan with a piece of clean glass or a tightly drawn piece of plastic wrap.

Each day put the pan out in the sun for about 8 hours. It takes about 3 days for the syrup to thicken. The berries can be gently turned over at the end of each day to insure even "cooking".

Put into cold, sterile jars and cover. You can sterilize the insides of the jar covers with brandy.

ROSE HIP JAM

Rose hips have a very high vitamin c content, many many more times higher than that of oranges, for example. The vitamin c content is highest in the late summer or fall when the rose hips are red, but you can pick them any time.

2 lbs. rose hips
1 lb. sugar
1 small orange

Chill rose hips, remove both stem and blossom ends, cut in half, and scoop out seeds. Bring 4 cups water to a boil in an enamel pan. Add the rose hips. Cover and cook about 30 minutes until the hips are very tender. Push through a sieve—let cool about 20 minutes.

Measure out 4 cups of pulp—that should be all of it—add 2 cups of sugar (or ½ the amount of pulp) and 1 small, very thinly sliced orange. Boil together about 20 minutes, stirring frequently.

Then test to see if it's done by dropping one tablespoon of it onto a cold plate. If a skin forms on the surface, it's ready. If it's not done, cook a few minutes more and test again.

You can remove the oranges if you want,

then pour into hot, sterilized jars and cover, or seal with paraffin.

* If you want to substitute honey for the sugar, it works equally as well. Add 1 cup of honey and taste the mixture before adding more. A Tablespoon or so of minced crystallized ginger is fun to add, too, if you happen to have some on hand.

* If you don't have any place to collect rose hips, you can buy them whole by mail-order from:

Walnut Acres
Penns Creek
Pennsylvania 17862
(ask for their free catalogue)

CRANBERRY-ORANGE SAUCE

This is good for the holidays, keeps forever, and everyone's impressed that you made it yourself even though it only takes 10 minutes to make.

In a saucepan combine:

1 c. sugar	½ c. orange juice
½ c. water	2 c. cranberries

Cover and cook over high heat until you can't hear the berries popping open any more – about 5 minutes.

Cool and refrigerate (preferably in a canning jar, for that down-home look).

BOYSENBERRY-APPLE JUICE

1 can frozen boysenberry juice
apple juice

Mix frozen boysenberry juice with water (follow directions on can).

Then mix apple juice with boysenberry juice — about half & half. Chill.

CRANBERRY JUICE

Thoroughly wash: 8 qts. cranberries
Then add : 6 qts. water to the berries in a large kettle.

Put on stove and boil until cranberries are mushy - skins will pop open -

Pour into a cheesecloth dripping bag, hang bag over kettle, and leave overnight.

To 4 qts. juice add 1 qt. sugar and 1 pt. water. Heat, but <u>don't</u> <u>boil</u>.

Bottle hot in sterile jars - pint jars work as well, if not better, than bottles.

* Cranberries have lots of vitamin C.

ORANGE JULIA

SERVES 2

1 ripe banana
2½ c. milk
3 heaping T. frozen orange juice concentrate
1 T. honey (or more to taste)

Mash bananas very thoroughly in a bowl. Stir in the orange juice, then the milk.

Pour into a quart jar with a top (or some kind of shaker) and add honey. Shake vigorously until you think it's well blended.

Refrigerate to chill and to let foam subside.

* If you have a blender, put all the ingredients (liquids first) into the blender container. Cover and process at "LIQUEFY" until smooth, about 5 seconds.

YOGRAPE DRINK

SERVES 1

2 oz. (1/4 c.) plain yogurt
4 oz. (1/2 c.) unsweetened grape juice

Mix together thoroughly, serve on ice.

MRS. B'S ICED TEA

4 qts. boiling water
10 t. tea
4 lemons
2 c. sugar
1 orange
bunch of fresh mint

Squeeze juice of 2 lemons into large pot. Cut other 2 lemons into wedges and add to pot along with the sugar and sliced orange. Stir a couple times.

Steep tea with mint separately for 5 minutes, then stir into the lemon mixture.

Strain when cool, pour into a large jug, & keep in the refrigerator.

Serve on ice with a mint sprig garnish.

* To uncloud tea that has been in the refrigerator, add 1/4 c. boiling water to 1 quart chilled tea.

FRENCH MOCHA

SERVES 6

¼ c. chocolate chips
¼ c. white corn syrup
¼ c. strong coffee
1 t. vanilla
½ pint heavy cream
1 qt. hot milk.

Melt chips with syrup over low heat.

When melted, add coffee gradually and blend well. Cool slightly and add vanilla.

Beat the heavy cream until thick, then slowly pour in chocolate mixture while beating at medium speed. Keep beating just until cream mounds. (Run your finger over the cream — when your finger-track remains, it's done.)

Spoon into a bowl and refrigerate at least 1 hour.

When ready to serve, scald the milk and pour into a warm coffee pot.

Spoon some of the chocolate into each cup and pour in milk. Each person can stir just before drinking.

GUACAMOLE

MAKES ABOUT 2 CUPS*

2 very ripe avocados
1 T. minced onion (or 1 t. onion powder)
1 T. lemon juice
mayonnaise

Peel and seed the two avocados. Mash with a fork and add onion and lemon juice.

Beat in about 4 T. mayonnaise to make a creamy mixture. Pack into a small bowl and cover with a thin film of mayonnaise (to keep avocado from getting black).

Keep in refrigerator until ready to use, then stir in mayonnaise.

Serve with Fritos as a dip thing, or on lettuce bed as a salad (* serves 4 as a salad).

TACOS AND ENCHILADAS

FOR 4

2 lbs. ground chuck
1 sm. can beef taco filling (if not available in your area, substitute a lot of chili powder).

1 medium onion, chopped
½ lb. cheddar cheese
2-3 lg. tomatoes
1 can pitted black olives (preferably chopped)
1 cup chopped lettuce
2 small avocados
1 cup bean sprouts
2 doz. corn tortillas (fresh, canned, or frozen)
1 can enchilada sauce
Salad oil or shortening
1 bottle or can taco sauce – at the risk of sounding dogmatic, if you have a choice get "Rosarita". If you can't get any at all, combine:
1 8 oz. can tomato sauce
1 fresh tomato, diced
½ med. onion, diced
2 t. chili powder
½ t. garlic salt

Simmer, covered, for about 1 hour, stirring frequently.

Preheat oven to 350°, then make the filling=

Brown the onion in 3 T. oil, add the meat and break it up and stir it so it browns all over. Then add the can of filling (or chili powder) - turn heat to low and let simmer while you do other things.

First other thing:

Grate the cheese or delegate that to one of the other three, while you:

heat about 1" of oil in a small skillet over medium-high heat. When hot, dip 1 dozen tortillas in, 1 at a time, using 2 forks or tongs to turn.

Think Quick!

It only takes about 30 seconds (15 each side) to cook a tortilla - otherwise it gets too stiff, like a Frito, and won't roll up.

Stack them on paper towels as you finish each one. When they're all done, place a spoonful each of meat filling and cheese on each of the tortillas, roll up and place seam side down in a shallow baking pan. Pour the enchilada sauce on top and sprinkle with a handful of cheese.

Put in the oven for ½ hour while you work on the tacos.

Next other thing:

If your cheese delegate is still handy, have him chop tomatoes, lettuce, olives, and avocado, and put them in separate little bowls on the table, along with the sprouts and the rest of the cheese, and the taco sauce. When everything is on the table except the meat filling (still simmering) and the enchiladas (about 5 minutes left to their ½ hr.) heat the oil again for the other dozen tortillas. Cook them the same as the others and stack with paper towels in between to drain. Some people like hard, crunchy taco shells — to make those, when a tortilla is done on one side, fold it in half leaving a 1" rounded bottom and support the top half with forks or tongs until it's hard enough to support itself. Then turn it over to cook the other side — about 2 minutes altogether.

When the tortillas are all cooked, put the meat filling in a bowl and take it and the stack of shells to the table.

Serve the enchiladas.

To construct a taco:

Hold the tortilla on the flat of your hand and start filling it with whatever you want (just a little of each or you'll never get it closed). Pour on a little taco sauce, roll up, and eat. Drink something very cold and start on your second.

This allows 3 enchiladas and 3 tacos for 4 people.

TAMALE PIE

SERVES 4

1 15 oz. can tamales
1 C. corn
1 8 oz. can tomato sauce
½ C. sliced black olives
1 C. crushed Fritos
1 C. shredded cheddar cheese

Peel the coverings off the tamales and place in a single layer in a greased baking dish.

Mix together the corn, sauce, and olives and pour over the tamales.

* Sprinkle Fritos and cheese over the top & bake at 375° for 25 minutes.

* This is not a traditional recipe — it's a whole other thing — but it's really good and easy to do.

WHOLE WHEAT SOPAIPILLAS

MAKES ABOUT 30 SMALL SOPAIPILLAS

4 c. whole wheat flour
4 t. baking powder
¼ c. shortening
2 t. salt
1 c. water (approx.)

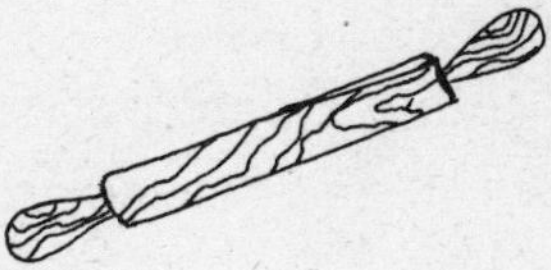

Mix dry ingredients together in a bowl. Cut in shortening, using a pastry blender or two knives (one held in each hand) until shortening is blended evenly. You can use your fingers, working quickly so as not to soften the shortening.

Add about 1 c. lukewarm water — more if you need it — and knead into a soft ball of dough.

Let rest for about 20 minutes in a covered bowl.

Roll dough about ⅛" thick on a lightly floured surface.

Cut into 2-3" squares or triangles.

Fry the sopaipillas in deep fat at 400°, immersing them several times when you first put them in so they'll puff up uniformly. If your fat isn't very deep (only 1-2" or so), spoon the fat over each sopaipilla several times 'til it puffs up. They should look like little pillows.

When the bottom side is golden brown, turn over and fry the top.

Serve piping hot with honey and butter.

* Sopaipillas are Mexican and are often served along with tacos. They are delicious little "biscuits" and are good for almost any occasion: breakfast, lunch, or dinner.

MEXICAN CHOCOLATE

SERVES 5-6

2 oz. unsweetened chocolate, grated
1/2 c. boiling water
2 c. milk
5 T. sugar
1 t. vanilla
1 c. heavy cream
pinch nutmeg
1 t. cinnamon
1 egg

Boil the chocolate in the water for 5 minutes.

Add milk, sugar, cream, and spices and cook in top of double boiler 1 hour, beating once every 10 minutes.

When ready to serve, beat the egg with the vanilla and dilute with a little hot chocolate. Then stir it slowly into the rest of the chocolate.

Beat very hard for 3 minutes until very frothy. Serve.

NOTES ON ORIENTAL COOKERY

Getting into oriental cooking (a very general kind of oriental cooking) is really something you ought to try. It is highly nutritious. The vegetables and meat are cooked quickly because they are bite-size; they are all cooked in the same pan, in only a small amount of liquid, none of which is discarded but instead becomes the sauce which binds together all the delicious flavours. The endless combinations and variations of vegetables and meat are entirely up to the cook's own inspiration.

These are general directions for a very general kind of cooking.

FIRST: Put the rice on to cook. (Brown rice is the most nutritious.)

SECOND: Mix together the following thickening ingredients, which won't be used until the very end:

2 T. cornstarch
2 t. soy sauce
1/4 c. cold water
} mix in a small bowl and put aside.

THIRD: Measure a cup of liquid and put aside. If you are not a vegetarian, the best liquid to use is real chicken or beef broth The next best is bouillon made from cubes or powder. Use chicken flavour for chicken or shrimp dishes, beef flavour for beef, pork, lamb, or veal dishes. If you are a vegetarian, the liquid can be water — tap, sprout, or vegetable-cooking water.

FOURTH: Cut raw meat (chicken, beef, veal, lamb, pork) into approx. 1/3" cubes or thin strips.
Dice a small heap of onions or scallions.
Mince a clove of garlic.
Slice a couple stalks of celery.
Dice some green pepper (opt.)
Slice some fresh mushrooms (opt.)

FIFTH: In a preheated, heavy, 10" frying pan (or a wok if you're lucky enough to have one) place: 2 T. cooking or salad oil (not olive oil)
1 t. salt
dash pepper
Add onion, garlic, mushrooms, & meat. Cook over med. heat, stirring a bit, for maybe 5 minutes.

SIXTH: Add celery and green pepper and cook and stir a couple more minutes.

SEVENTH: Add 1 c. stock, broth, bouillon, or water (you set it aside in #3).

NOW: Small pieces of beef, chicken, and fresh or frozen shrimp cook fairly quickly and would be nearly done.

Other meats need to simmer, covered, 5 or 10 minutes longer. You want to add the vegetables at such times that they will not overcook. They should be slightly on the raw side. Frozen peas or green beans or chopped fresh broccoli are good choices & cook quickly. Fresh peas and fresh green beans take longer.

EIGHTH: When meat and vegetables are nearly done, add the cornstarch mixture. Stir constantly until juice thickens.

NINTH: Add some salad-type stuff: tomato quarters, raw caulifloweretttes, sliced cabbage, sprouted seeds.

Serve immediately with the hot rice & tea. Pass around soy sauce & duck sauce.

The recipes on the following pages are simply variations on the theme. They may seem redundant, but may give you a few tested dishes to start out with.

CHINESE SPARERIBS

SERVES 2

2 lb. pork ribs, cut in individual pieces
1 onion, chopped (or 4 scallions)
4 T. brown sugar
4 T. vinegar
1 t. salt
5 T. soy sauce

Bring a big pot of water to a boil and add ribs. Let boil for 10 minutes. Then drain and dry the ribs. This removes most of the excess fat & partially cooks the meat.

Heat 6 T. margarine in a large skillet, then add the ribs and fry until very brown, turning once, about 25 minutes. Add onions.

Blend together sugar, vinegar, salt, and soy sauce and pour over ribs. Cover and cook about 15 more minutes until ribs are thoroughly coated and sauce is absorbed.

Serve with duck sauce.

TEMPURA

Batter mix : 1 c. flour
1 c. water
1 egg (or 2 yolks)
1 t. sugar
dash salt (optional)
½ t. baking powder (optional— but it does help make the batter puff up more)

Break egg into bowl. Gradually add 1 cup water while stirring with a fork.

Using both a stirring and a chopping motion, add the flour, sugar (and opt. ingredients).

Stir only until flour is blended — do not over-blend. Batter should be slightly lumpy.

Cover and put in refrigerator for 15 minutes.

Bite-size meat, fish, vegetables, and even fruits can be dipped in tempura batter and deep fried:

- celery
- fresh asparagus
- ¼" green pepper rings
- unpeeled, sliced zucchini
- sliced eggplant
- sliced sweet potato
- carrots
- water chestnuts
- ¼" sliced mushrooms
- tomatoes
- artichoke hearts
- string beans
- whole clams, oysters, & shrimp
- fish filets
- bits of chicken

The ingredients should be thoroughly dried, then dipped in batter, then deep-fried quickly (preferably in peanut oil) at 375°.

Drain and serve with lemon, soy sauce, or Sweet and Sour Sauce (p.186).

✱ Apples, pears, and bananas are tasty fruits to use. Cut into pieces, dry, fry, drain & sprinkle with powdered sugar.

SWEET AND SOUR SAUCE

MAKES 2 ½ CUPS

Make a paste of: 2 T. cornstarch
½ c. chicken broth
2 T. soy sauce

Melt in a heavy pan: 2 T. margarine
Add: 1 c. chicken broth
¾-1 c. chunks of green pepper
canned pineapple chunks—as much as you want

Cover and simmer 5 minutes.
Add cornstarch paste.
Add: ½ c. vinegar
¾ c. pineapple juice or syrup from can
½ c. brown sugar
½ t. salt
¼ t. ginger
Simmer, stirring constantly, until mixture thickens.

A handful of cherry tomatoes can be stirred in at the end.

*This sauce is particularly good with shrimp Tempura - serve it with hot boiled rice.

CHICKEN AND ALMONDS

SERVES 2-3

Make a paste of: 2 T. cornstarch
1/4 C. chicken broth
2 T. soy sauce

Heat 2 T. vegetable oil in a large, heavy skillet.
Add: 1 onion, thinly sliced
8 large mushrooms, sliced
Sauté about 2 minutes, stirring frequently.
Add: 1 1/2 boneless chicken breasts, cut into pieces
2 ribs celery, cut on diagonal into pieces
1 8 oz. can bamboo shoots, drained
1 1/2 t. brown sugar or honey
Stir and cook until chicken is tender.
Stir in cornstarch paste, simmer & stir until sauce thickens.
Stir in 1/2 c. almonds.
Serve on hot boiled rice with soy sauce.

DICED PORK WITH ALMONDS AND VEGETABLES

SERVES 4

Blanch and chop 1/4 c. almonds

Cook in 2 T. vegetable oil until golden brown. Drain.

Dice 2 c. carrots.

Shell 1 lb. peas.

Steam in a small saucepan until tender about 5 minutes

Heat 4 T. oil and 1 t. salt in a 10" frying pan.

Cut 1 lb. lean pork into 1/3" cubes, and cook in frying pan over med. heat until golden brown.

Dice and add 2 c. celery.

Add 1/2 c. chicken broth.

Add cooked carrots and peas, cover pan, and simmer about 5 minutes until meat is tender.

Blend together and add: 2 T. cornstarch
2 t. soy sauce
1/3 c. vegetable water

Stir constantly until juice thickens and mixture is hot. Stir in almonds.

Serve immediately with boiled rice.

CHINESE VEGETABLES

Make sauce thickener by mixing together 2 T. cornstarch with 3/4 c. stock (chicken, vegetable).

Cut up some onions and mushrooms.

Sauté them in 2 T. butter or margarine for a couple minutes.

Cut up some washed and chilled broccoli, cabbage, carrots, bok choy, green beans, yams, sprouts, anything you want, really.

Add to the onions and mushrooms, turn up the heat and stir constantly for 2 minutes.

Reduce heat, add about 2 t. soy sauce, some pepper, brown sugar or honey to taste, pinch of basil and a small pinch of tarragon.

Add sauce thickener, stir, cover, and simmer for about 5 minutes.

Serve on hot rice.

* For chop suey, add bits of meat.

ALMOND COOKIES

1 c. white sugar
1 c. lard (makes cookies much lighter than margarine)
3 c. flour
3 hard-boiled egg yolks
1 t. baking powder
1 ½ t. almond extract
1 raw egg white
whole blanched almonds

Cream the sugar with the lard. Mash the yolk and add to the sugar/lard. Then add the extract and the flour a little at a time, working it in with your hands — the dough will be very stiff.

Break off a little bit of dough at a time and roll into a small ball. Press flat to make a ½" cookie. Dip a whole blanched almond into the egg white and press into the top of the cookie.

Bake in a pre-heated 375° oven until golden brown (about 8 minutes).

TABLE OF DIVIDED MEASURES

Speck	less than 1/8 t.
1/3 of 1/4 t.	pinch
1/3 of 1/2 t.	pinch
1/2 of 1/4 t.	1/8 t.
1/2 of 3/4 t.	3/8 t.
3 t.	1 T.
1/3 of 1 T.	1 t.
1/3 of 2 T.	2 t.
1/3 of 5 T.	1 T. and 2 t.
1/3 of 7 T.	2 T. and 1 t.
1/2 of 1 T.	1 1/2 t.
1/2 of 3 T.	1 T. and 1 1/2 t.
1/2 of 5 T.	2 T. and 1 1/2 t.
1/2 of 7 T.	3 T. and 1/2 t.
2 T.	1/8 c.
4 T.	1/4 c.
5 T. and 1 t.	1/3 c.
8 T.	1/2 c.
12 T.	3/4 c.
16 T.	1 c.
1/3 of 1/4 c.	1 T. and 1 t.
1/3 of 1/3 c.	1 T. and 2 1/3 t.
1/3 of 1/2 c.	2 T. and 2 t.
1/3 of 2/3 c.	3 T. and 1 2/3 t.
1/3 of 3/4 c.	1/4 c.

1/2 of 1/4 c.	2 T. (1/8 c.)
1/2 of 1/3 c.	2 T. and 2 t.
1/2 of 1/2 c.	1/4 c.
1/2 of 2/3 c.	1/3 c.
1/2 of 3/4 c.	6 T.
2 c.	1 pint
2 pints.	1 quart
1 quart.	4 c.
4 quarts	1 gallon
16 oz. (1 pint).	1 lb.

INDEX